I0149573

Victory Thoughts by
Moses Johnson Sr. & Vivian M. Johnson

ISBN-13: 978-0692537749 (Custom)
ISBN-10: 0692537740

BISAC: Religion / Christian Life / Spiritual Growth

Printed in the United States of America

Unless otherwise noted all scripture
is from The Holy Bible

Mackey Productions
"Catch the Vision of Victory & Never Give Up"

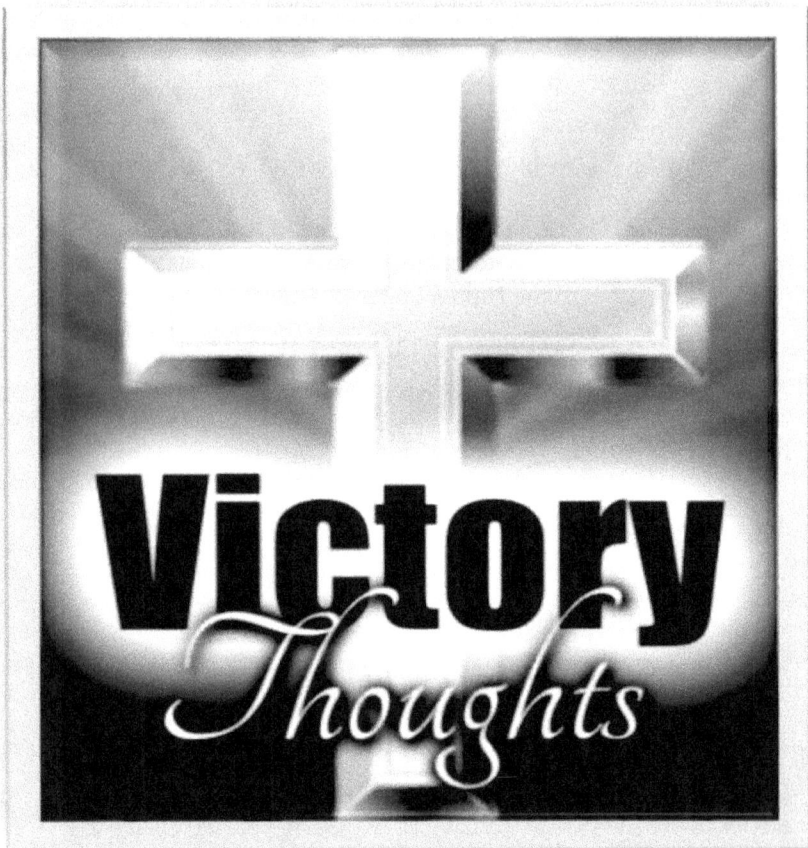

Stories, Testimonies & Life Lessons

Moses Johnson Sr. & Vivian M. Johnson

Share Some Love

House of Prayer Evangelistic Ministries Inc.

We pray that as you read you will feel our hearts,
our prayers and the spirit of the Lord.

Our Website is:
www.sharesomelove2.weebly.com

Our Face Book Group is:
Share Some Love Group

Our Daily Encouragement Page on Face Book is:
Share Some Love 2

Follow Us on Twitter

Table of Contents

Chapter 4

Chapter 5

Chapter 6

Special Dedication

In Loving Memory of
Rev. Dr. Arthur L. Mackey Sr.
Former Pastor of the Mt. Sinai Baptist Church
Roosevelt, New York

He loved to laugh,
tell stories, and to share.
He loved to testify of God's goodness!!!
He loved God, his family and people!!!
Gone, but never forgotten!!!

April 29, 1938 – October 29, 1999

Our Thanks

First and foremost we give thanks to the Lord without whom none of this would be possible.

The LORD hath done great things for us;
whereof we are glad.
Psalm 126:3

There are so many people who have touched our lives and been a blessing to us over the years. We extend our heartfelt love and thanks to you all.

To Our Children
We Love You All Very Much!!!
Kameisha Johnson & family, Shauna Johnson-Scheffler
& family, Natalia Johnson, Kwayne Johnson & family,
Jeneal Johnson Peele & Family,
Akheam Johnson and Moses Johnson Jr.

To Our Grandchildren
Jazmine Gonzales, Lorenzo Peterson,
Curtys (CJ), Aubriana, Curshau & Kadin Scheffler, Chloe & Kayson
Johnson

Special Thanks to
My Mother & My Mother in Love
Rev. Dr. Frances W. Mackey

In Loving Memory of
Rev. Dr. Arthur L. Mackey Sr., Ms. Murna Lane,
Mr. Alphonso Johnson, Mr. Wilbert Stewart,
Ms. Hazel Graham, Ms. Delrose McDonald,
Mr. Paul Beckford and Mr. Mark Beckford
Mr. Alfred Williams. Mr. Joseph Williams Jr.

Special Thanks to My Sisters

Mrs. Merlena Stewart and Mrs. Angela Williams are two towers of inspiration and strength whom God placed in our lives to inspire and strengthen us.

Special Thanks to Our Families

Our brothers and sisters, nieces, nephews, cousins, aunts and uncles, our god-children, spiritual children, Mackey family, Williams family, Buckner family, Kay family, Woodside Family, Jackson family, Lane family, Johnson family, Peele Family, Scheffler Family, Williams Family (Jamaica, WI), Stewart Family (Jamaica, WI), Beckford Family (Jamaica, WI).

Special Thanks to

Pastor Arthur Mackey Jr. & Elder Brenda Mackey and family, the Mt. Sinai Baptist Church Family of Roosevelt, New York; Pastors Tyrone & Frances Woodside and family, the Perfecting Love Church family, Winter Haven, Florida; Deacon Curtis Womack & Trustee Diane Womack & Family; Lady Charmaine Day; Pastor Darryle Bass & Lady Annette Bass, the Ultimate Praise Ministries of Bear, Delaware; Sis. Josephine Williams, Chief Apostle J. Raymond Mackey & Elder Brenda Mackey, Tabernacle of Joy Churches Worldwide; Rev. Elijah Mackey, Elder Dora Smith, Elder & Attorney Lester Mackey & Dr. Sharon Mackey, Bishop E. L. Woodside & Evangelist Eva Woodside, Share Some Love House of Prayer Evangelistic Ministries.

Special Thanks to

Pastor Arthur L. Mackey Jr. and Mackey Productions. We thank God for you. Thank you for encouraging us. Mentoring us and making the publishing of this book possible.

To My Husband Moses
(From Vivian)

Moses (Honey),

When I dragged my feet on the project you took the mantle and ran with the vision. You took the necessary steps to get first project going and encouraged me to hurry up and get the second book done. You opened the door for our creative writing ministry to be shared with the world. You encouraged me spiritually to move to the next level. You helped me to stir up the gift of God within me. You bring out the best in me!

Moses my love, you are a true man of prayer, vision and commitment. You are full of passion and purpose. I love you with my whole heart. I thank God for you every day of my life!!! You have blessed my world with sunshine, laughter, music and gave me what I longed for most. A family of my own. Thank you for making me feel loved and appreciated. You are a great Dad, a wonderful Husband, a dynamic Teacher and Preacher of the Gospel. I know that God will continue to use you for His glory !!!

To My Wife Vivian
(From Moses)

Vivian (My Love), You came alongside to help me. You worked with me to create, mold and shape the vision God gave me. You are anointed. I love you with all my heart!!!

You are a loving wife, a caring and dedicated mother and a reat homemaker. You care for our family and make sure we are well taken care of. You are a strong woman of God. Saved, sanctified and filled with the Holy Spirit. You are richly blessed with godly wisdom, knowledge and understanding. You are a hard working woman with rich life experience. My Love, May God continue to bless you and keep you all the days of your life.

There are so many who have
touched our lives in so many ways.
We cannot list you all but know
That your lives, ministries
and friendship have been a
blessing in our lives.

We love you and thank God for you!!!

Share Some Love
House of Prayer Evangelistic Ministries Inc.

Introduction

The inspiration for this book came to me as I lay in my hospital bed after having surgery. I was praying and asking the Lord some questions about our future. He spoke to my spirit and said "Use what's in your hand."

I said, "Lord I don't understand." He showed me the picture of a book and said, "Tell your story". He layed it out in my mind plain for me to see. God gave me the vision.

And the LORD answered me, and said, Write the vision, and make *it* plain upon tables, that he may run that readeth it. **Habakkuk 2:2.**

"Victory Thoughts' is filled with personal stories, testimonies and life lessons.

We prayed, listened and waited for the Lord to speak to our hearts and give us the words for each story we shared. This is not a collection of random thoughts but it is under the leading, guiding and direction of the Holy Spirit.

Our prayer is that you will be encouraged as you see how God has worked in our lives for his glory. We pray that you will be encouraged, strengthened, motivated and inspired.

We pray that the Lord will touch hearts and change lives for his glory! What He's done for others He will do for you too! Praise God! When you release your heart and put your life in God's hands. He can change your life for the better!

One of our favorite scriptures is **Romans 8:28**. And we know that all things work together for good to those who love God, to those who are the called according to His purpose.

This is a book for leaders, overcomers, those who have a vision. For those who want a better life. For those who dare to dream. For those who believe there is more to life.

There is a word of encouragement, strength, hope and direction for everyone who reads this book. This book is for every person who wants or needs a change in their life. Those looking for motivation and inspiration. Those who need a word from the Lord.

This book details how all things have worked together for our good. We are overcomers. We are more than conquerors. We walk in victory. It may not always be good but it will work together for your good if you trust God in the midst of it! Be blessed!!!

Chapter 1

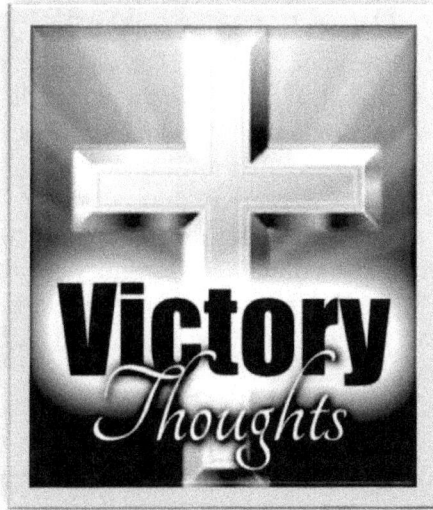

Family Blessings
& Your Inheritance

In this chapter we start by honoring our parents & sharing how God worked in their lives. We tell about Abraham struggles, blessings and promises from God.

We Come From Strong People

Rev. Dr. Arthur L. Mackey Sr.

Rev. Dr. Arthur L. Mackey Sr. was born on April 29, 1938 in Brooklyn, New York to Rev. Walter R. Mackey Sr. and Dora Hill Mackey. He was 3 lbs. 2 oz. His first bed was a dresser drawer. He was sickly and his parents were told to take him to the country until he died.

His family moved to Roosevelt, New York on Long Island where his father built the Mt. Sinai Baptist Church. His parents were affectionately called "Ma Mack" and Big Daddy" by everyone. They reared six sons (Walter, Larry, Arthur, John, James and Elijah), one daughter (Inez) and many foster children.

My dad was a tall skinny boy with crossed eyes and wore eyeglasses. He loved to work in the garden and preach to the cabbage. Those who thought he would never amount to anything were greatly surprised.

He became a Minister and went to Virginia Union University where he looked across the campus and met the love of his life Frances Williams. He was never shy about sharing how much he loved his wife and family (I guess that's where I get it from). He became the Pastor of Mt. Sinai Baptist Church and pastored for 34 years. My father was a dedicated father of three children. Frances Mackey Woodside, Vivian Mackey Johnson and Arthur Mackey Jr. All three children and their spouses are in ministry today. He loved to spend time with his grandchildren, watch them play, tell them stories, and he loved to take them on trips to Pennsylvania Dutch Country or whatever trip they were going on.

As a young child I remember the day a police officer knocked on our door late at night. They asked my father to come help with a riot that was going on. God used him as a negotiator. That was the start of him getting involved politically. His heart, his goal, his mission was to help others and he fulfilled his life's purpose.

My father became an advocate for the community and civil rights. He fought for those less fortunate locally and nationally. He did his part to fight social and racial discrimination. He helped to start the Nassau County Black Clergy which fought to help minorities. He was a part of the Eastern Baptist Association of New York. He started Job Programs, Food Feeding Programs, Housing Programs, and helped countless people in his lifetime. He helped to open doors for many leaders and other pastors to walk through.

My Dad was the first Black President of the Nassau County Medical Center. As a teenager I loved walking the halls of the hospital with him. Everyone saying – "Hi Rev. Mackey", "Can I talk to you Rev. Mackey?" "I need some help Rev. Mackey". He always stopped to talk or gave his card and said – "Call me at the office". He negotiated the deal for the hospitals Heart Program with the New York Governor. He met with Senators, Congressmen, and Presidents. Yet, he remained humble.

In addition to being a full time Pastor he worked for the Nassau County Commission on Human Rights. He served as the Director for the Nassau County Job Development Center. He helped many people get jobs and also overlooked the youth job program. There's not enough room or paper to tell all the things my Dad did to help others.

My father achieved and received many honors. His motto was: "If I can help somebody then my living shall not be in vain." Never doubt what God can do in your life when you trust him. After his passing the street where the church is was renamed "Rev. Dr. A. L. Mackey Sr. Ave" (formerly Frederick Ave.). One of the local parks was also renamed after him. Roosevelt Park was renamed Rev. Dr. Arthur L. Mackey Sr. Park.

My father was named as one the top 100 Most Influential Long Islanders of the Century. He was noted as "Someone who made a difference". Many things have been said about my father but the one thing that stands out is God used him for his glory!!! Look at God!!! That 3lb 2 oz. baby boy turned into a Great Man of God. 6 feet 3 inches, and plenty of meat on his bones. He was always motivated by the fact that people said he wouldn't make it. BUT HE DID!!! We thank God for the many, many seeds he planted in the lives of others. Thank God for him being a living testimony!

Rev. Dr. Frances W. Mackey

Rev. Dr. Frances W. Mackey was born on October 24, 1938 in Washington, DC to Joseph Freeman Williams Sr. and Eunice Rock Williams. After the death of her father at 29 years old she and her brothers (Joseph Junior and Alfred) were sent to live with family in Woodford, Virginia.

My mother came from a humble background. She grew up on the family farm which was 150 acres inherited from slavery. The home resembled a modern log cabin with no running water and several other modern amenities missing.

It came complete with an outhouse and the family grave yard just down the road. My mother always said she accepted the Lord at an early age at Addie Alsop's well.

Her mother remarried Mr. Ennis Buckner and she had two more brothers (James and Albert) and a sister (Vivian aka Aunt Ann after whom I am named).

At a young age she left home to find a better life for herself. She ended up living with her foster mother who helped her through high school and prepared her for college. She received a college scholarship from the Virginia Minister's Wives.

She attended Virginia Union University in Richmond, Virginia. She lived in the home of the University's Chancellor and his wife. She did work around the house while attending college. There she met a young preacher named Arthur Mackey. She later married that young preacher from New York who everyone called "Mackey".

Together they built a family. They had three children: Pastor Frances Mackey Woodside, Elder Vivian Mackey Johnson and Pastor Arthur L. Mackey Jr. and helped rear their niece Lydia Mackey Walker.

My mother was a Christian Education major and wanted to be a Missionary. Instead she moved to Roosevelt, New York and used her skills and talents to be a blessing. My mother served as a Pastor's wife for 34 years

My mother worked as a teacher at the Roosevelt Head Start program until illness. She became a fulltime Homemaker. She is a Friend, Mother, Grandmother, Teacher, Organizer, she is an Ordained Minister, Pastoral Counselor and Administrator par excellent. She was teased as a young girl because she had holes in her stockings. "Look at Frances, she's running for President". They were prophesying- She became President of the Local, State, National and International Minister's Wives and Widows Association. She has received many honors and made many achievements. Look at God!

Murna Merle Lane

Murna Meryl Lane was born on January 21, 1939 in Kingston, Jamaica, West Indies. Her mother, Mrs. Daisy Lane died during child birth. Her father, Mr. Munsell Lane married again and had additional children.

As a single parent of five daughters and one son (Elder Moses Johnson Sr.). She experienced many hardships. Homelessness and poverty tried to take their toll but she was an overcomer and more than a conqueror.

Ms. Murna was a smart businesswoman and put her skills to work. In America she would be called an "Entrepreneur". She had her own successful business.
In the midst of political unrest and violence she survived. She worked and fought hard to secure a home for her family.

After a fire where she was living, she was finally able to buy her own home. This was a great accomplishment for her.

Ms. Murna was a beautiful, lively, light skinned woman with a zest and love for life, people and family. Her children and grandchildren called her "Mama". As the matriarch of the family she shared what she had and stretched her resources to feed her large family.

She got saved and became a member of the Church of God of Prophecy. She attended church every Sunday and sat in the same pew. She was a prayer warrior. Her prayers were one of the driving force in turning Moses' life around.

When my mom went home to be with the Lord I asked for two things: Her Bible and her hymnbook. Today that Bible and hymnbook are in are our home. Having them makes me feel close to her and gives me a connection to my mother that will last forever.

I remember my mother singing while working in the kitchen and when she did the laundry. Her favorite scripture was Psalm 91 and her favorite hymn was Amazing Grace.

Through her hard work and dedication her children followed in her footsteps. My two older sisters became Entrepreneurs, another a Bank Manager and one a Cosmetologist (one of my sisters died before her first birthday anniversary).

I, her only son, Elder Moses Johnson Sr. worked in Grace Kennedy Central Laboratory, and taught English Language and Science at a prominent high school in Jamaica, West Indies. I later became an Ordained Minister.

My mother, Ms. Murna Lane left a lasting legacy with her children and grandchildren. Our prayers for our children are never in vain. God will always make a difference in our lives when we yield ourselves to him.

Alphonso Alpheus Johnson

Alphonso Alpheus Johnson was born to William Johnson and Lillian Walker Johnson in Westmoreland, Jamaica in April of 1938. He was the only child and his father died when he was a toddler. He was an only child and the father of many children.

He was a tailor by trade and a businessman. He owned a restaurant in the tourist resort of Negril Jamaica. He was well known in the tourism industry in Jamaica. His restaurant serviced the tourist industry in Jamaica as well.

He made many friends with people from other countries. His restaurant featured many pictures with tourists from all over the world. His menu included delicious dishes from North and South America, Europe, Asia and the West Indies, mainly Jamaica.

Spending time with my father gave me the opportunity to learn many life lessons about being a man.

A Family Blessing

We thank God for bringing us together. We thank God for our parents and our heritage. We thank God for him working in the lives of each family member. We thank God for what he has done in the past and what he will do in the future. We pray God's blessings upon our children and our children's children. In Jesus name. Amen.

II Kings 2:9
And it came to pass, when they were gone over, that Elijah said unto Elisha, Ask what I shall do for thee, before I be taken away from thee. And Elisha said, I pray thee, let a double portion of thy spirit be upon me.

Psalm 78:5-6
For he established a testimony in Jacob, and appointed a law in Israel, which he commanded our fathers, that they should make them known to their children: That the generation to come might know them, even the children which should be born; who should arise and declare them to their children:

Jeremiah 29:11
For I know the plans I have for you" this is the LORD's declaration "plans for your welfare, not for disaster, to give you a future and a hope".

Numbers 6:24-26
The Lord bless you and keep you; The Lord make His face shine upon you, and be gracious to you; The Lord lift up His countenance upon you, And give you peace.

Proverbs 13:22A
A good man leaves an inheritance to his children's children.

I don't know if they remember but with our older children one day during family time we had a special blessing ceremony. We shared verbal blessings upon them and gave each one a special booklet made just for them with a written blessing.

All of our children are strong, unique and blessed. As parents it is our responsibility to call forth the things of God in their life. To pray and speak God's blessing over them.

We all do not have the same experiences in life but we can all find something good in our lives to stop and thank God for.

Lord, as we live our lives from day to day help us to plant good seeds in the lives of others. Help us to live so the next generation will want to love you, serve you and can't live without you.

Expect God to Bless You!

How many times have you looked back over your life and seen where the Lord has brought you from? How many times have you gone through a hardship and asked God to bring you out and deliver you? How many times have you looked beyond the circumstances with eyes of faith?

How many times have you said – "I know the Lord has his hands on me and I know the Lord is going to bless me." Have you prayed and said – "Lord, change me." Change my attitude, change my thoughts, one day at a time, one thought at a time. How many times have you thought, I love you Lord, I am serving you Lord, not because of any good thing on my part my Father but through your merciful kindness, I expect you to bless me Lord.

Matthew 19:26. But Jesus beheld them, and said unto them, with men this is impossible; but with God all things are possible.

Don't Let Go of Your Blessing!

Jacob Wrestles with God
Genesis 32:23-31 (Holman Christian Bible)

Jacob was left alone, and a man wrestled with him until daybreak. When the man saw that He could not defeat him, He struck Jacob's hip socket as they wrestled and dislocated his hip. Then He said to Jacob, "Let Me go, for it is daybreak." But Jacob said, "I will not let you go unless you bless me." "What is your name?" the man asked. "Jacob," he replied. "Your name will no longer be Jacob," He said. "It will be Israel because you have struggled with God and with men and have prevailed." Then Jacob asked Him, "Please tell me your name." But He answered, "Why do you ask my name?" And He blessed him there. Jacob then named the place Peniel, "For I have seen God face to face," he said, "and I have been delivered." The sun shone on him as he passed by Penuel limping because of his hip.

Next Generation Blessings!

Genesis 12:1-3. Now the LORD had said unto Abram, Get thee out of thy country, and from thy kindred, and from thy father's house, unto a land that I will shew thee: And I will make of thee a great nation, and I will bless thee, and make thy name great; and thou shalt be a blessing: And I will bless them that bless thee, and curse him that curse thee: and in thee shall all families of the earth be blessed.

The Blessings of Abraham

1. The first blessing is Genesis 12:1
   unto a land that I will shew thee
2. Blessing number two. Genesis 12:2
   And I will make of thee a great nation
3. Blessing number three in Genesis 12:2
   and I will bless thee

4. Blessing number four. Genesis 12:2
   and make thy name great
5. Blessing number five Genesis 12:2
   and thou shalt be a blessing
6. Blessing number six of Abraham Genesis 12:3
   And I will bless them that bless thee
7. The seventh blessing of Abraham. Genesis 12:3
   and in thee shall all families of the earth be blessed

Accept Your Inheritance

When you are a Christian, you are the seed of Abraham! That means everything God promised him belongs to you. It has been passed down to you through Jesus. Abraham's blessing is your inheritance! It has been given to you by the Word of God. We must read and study God's Word that we may know what He has promised and how to receive our blessing.

Romans 8:16 -17. The Spirit himself testifies with our spirit that we are God's children. Now if we are children, then we are heirs—heirs of God and co-heirs with Christ, if indeed we share in his sufferings in order that we may also share in his glory.

LIFE LESSONS

- No matter where you come from or what your past is God has a plan and a purpose for your life.
- No matter what we experience in life we can always find some good.
- Looking back at our parent's lives we are blessed by seeing God at work in them and through them.
- God used these ordinary people to strengthen us through their stories, testimonies and life's lessons.
- If God can work the impossible in our lives he can work in yours.
- Are you speaking God's blessing over your family?
- Are you passing on God's Word to the next generation?
- Can your children see God at work in your life?
- Pray and ask God to bless your family.

Chapter 2

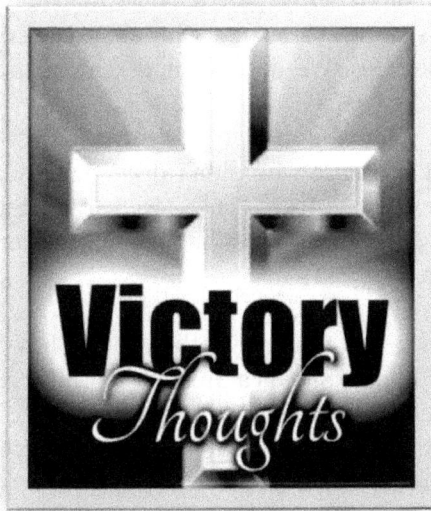

Friendship, Evangelism & Hospitality

Reaching out and sharing the love of Jesus
in ordinary ways. Loving God, loving people
and sharing God's Word.

The Ministry of Hospitality

My father would tell us to always set an extra plate or two at the table every Sunday for dinner. My parents love to have "company". Every Sunday there was always someone who stayed over at our house for dinner between services. We lived right next door to the church in the parsonage.

It was convenient for those who didn't drive or have a ride back to the afternoon service to stay over. There were two church mothers who stayed with us every Sunday. They ministered to our family and we in turn ministered to them.

I can't tell you how many times my father said, "I'll be right back." When he returned he had the family meal from KFC. Chicken, biscuits, mac and cheese, string beans and of course it came with a cake. Whatever my parents had whether it was little or much they spread it on the table, blessed it and shared with everyone.

My mom used to have an expression "Open Heart, Open Home." My parents lived for God daily in simple ways and they passed that along to their children.

We each have the gift of hospitality in our own way. However, I do believe my sister is the Queen of hospitality. The Lord really uses her to minister to others through event planning.

We have many opportunities to be a witness to others through friendship and hospitality. Being a living testimony for others to see in ordinary ways.

Lord, help me to let my light shine daily in ordinary ways that others may be drawn to you as they see Christ in us. God uses the gift of hospitality.

Hebrews 13:2. Be not forgetful to entertain strangers: for thereby some have entertained angels unawares.

LIFE LESSONS

- Sharing a hot cup of tea with a smile.
- Sharing some banana bread.
- Sharing a listening and compassionate ear.
- Sharing a simple prayer.
- Sharing a helping hand.
- Find ways to show you care.
- When was the last time you entertained in your home?
- Do you see the opportunity to share the gift of hospitality with others in your life?
- What difference would the gift of hospitality make in your ministry? In your home? In your personal relationships?

Who Can I Show Hospitality?

1._____

2._____

3._____

4._____

Bring Them In

Our older son has a way with people. As a young man he said he had to work hard at making friends. His smile and manner tend to draw people to him.

Our daughter was graduating from High School. There were not enough tickets so everyone went to the graduation and I stayed home to cook and prepare for the party afterwards.

Not everyone who was invited showed up. It was a nice little gathering of a few friends and a few parents. However I had cooked loads of food.

Our son jumped on his bike and said he would be right back. All of a sudden it was like a scene from out of a movie. I could see the children coming over the hill and down the green grass.

They were headed for my house. I looked out and saw my front porch loaded with teenagers.

Our son was just about to bring everyone in my house when I stopped him at the door. I said give me a minute. Another mom helped me and we made a line through the front door and back to the porch. All the teenagers inside moved outside and we had one big party going on.

We fed everyone and still had some left. Our son wanted his sister's party to be a success and for her to feel loved. That was his gift to her.

He went out into the area we lived and compelled his friends to come. He was doing what I call Friendship Evangelism.

When your children are young God will allow you to see their talents, gifts, and abilities if you ask Him.

It is our job as parents to encourage them. Our son has favor with people and a compassionate heart. God is going to use him for his glory! We see God in our children's lives. We see Him working in them and through them for His glory!

Luke 14:23
And the Lord said unto the servant, Go out into the highways and hedges, and compel them to come in, that my house may be filled.

My husband used to be the Director of the Evangelism ministry at our home church in New York. I remember one day when doing street witnessing Pastor said "Let's go in the bar". You had to see the faces when we went in there. They were shocked to say the least.

Many people greeted the Pastor and told him "I'll be at church on Sunday." He said on Sunday, "If anyone told you they saw me in the bar this week they were right. We were witnessing and we're going out next week with sandwiches to hit the streets again."

He took it literally when the Bible told us to go out and compel them to come. That's how we were trained as ministers and that's the example we follow.

LIFE LESSONS

- Many people are a little apprehensive when it comes to Evangelism and Street Witnessing.
- It's simply inviting a friend to your house.
- God wants us to go out and bring them in!
- We need to get moving in obedience to the Lord!!!

How Can I Evangelize?

1._____

2._____

3._____

4._____

Friendship Evangelism

As the Coordinators of Vision of Victory Ministries at the church one of our projects was Friendship Sunday. We encouraged others to bring a friend to church.

Many people participated and we gave gifts to those who brought a lot of friends or the most people. This also gave our children the opportunity to invite their friends.

We usually had a dinner downstairs afterward. It was one of the ways we implemented low key evangelism. Our job was to go out and bring the people in. Once they were there Pastor did his job and preached the Word.

When was the last time you invited a friend or family member to attend church service with you?

I remember thinking at one point how can someone stay away from church? It's done one Sunday at a time. One service at a time.

Is there someone you have missed from church? Is there someone who never comes to church? Extend the love of Jesus through Friendship Evangelism.

And let us consider one another in order to stir up love and good works, not forsaking the assembling of ourselves together, as *is* the manner of some, but exhorting *one another,* and so much the more as you see the Day approaching —**Hebrews 10:24-25.**

LIFE LESSONS

- Don't be afraid to reach out.
- Reach out this week and invite someone to church.
- If they need a ride pick them up and bring them.
- Sheep make Sheep.
- Reach out and touch those people who the Lord has put within your area of influence.

Ordinary Things

The ice cream truck would come around every day at the same time. We usually didn't have much money for ice cream and candy.

Our father didn't want us to stand out and be upset because we weren't like the others who could afford ice cream every day.
Our dad went to the super market and bought us ice and chocolate fudge pops. When the ice cream man came around my parents told us to come inside and get ice cream.

The best part was they bought enough for us to give our friends too. If someone didn't have the money they didn't have to go without. They just came to our back door and stood on line and received ice cream.

God can use small ordinary things to bless you and God can use you (if you let him) to bless others as well. Even if it's just a small thing like ice cream. The principles remain the same.

And my God shall supply all your need according to His riches in glory by Christ Jesus –**Philippians 4:19**

LIFE LESSONS

- God will supply your needs.
- God will make your money stretch.
- Think not just about yourself but how to share with others. Think ministry.
- People will not always accept you, learn to deal with it. Know who you are in Christ and go with it.
- Lord, help us to teach our children how to share and care on a daily basis.

Ordinary Things God Can Use

1._____

2._____

Be an Encourager

As a young person I can count the times in my life when someone took the time to speak into my life and encourage me in the work I was doing. I remember one of the church mothers asking me to do devotional for Women's Day in the afternoon for the Youth Service. I was scared. I practiced songs and led the worship. It changed my life. She told me I could do it. My parents told me I could do it.

A bit older I remember one of the Deacons telling me he was blessed by my singing. I know people who are blessed tremendously and can really sing. Next to them I thought I couldn't sing at all. That word though encouraged me and moved me to another level. Another Deacon Friend told me if I made a record he would buy it. I believe it was a great encouragement and it helped boost my confidence.

In my life my greatest encouragers have been my mother, father, brother, sister and my husband. I watched and learned from my mother the practice, art and gift of encouragement.

Sometimes all we need is an encouraging word to help us along the way. "I enjoyed that prayer, you read the scripture very well. You did great."

It's good that there are so many people who are positive, and praise and encourage others? Don't hold it back.

ROMANS 1:12 NLT.
WHEN WE GET TOGETHER, I WANT TO ENCOURAGE YOU IN YOUR FAITH, BUT I ALSO WANT TO BE ENCOURAGED BY YOU.

LIFE LESSONS
- Ask God to show you ways to encourage and how to bless others daily.
- Go ahead and be a blessing!!! You never know what it will do to lift someone else's spirit.

How Can I Help???

I remember when my niece and nephews were young. My father would go over to my sister's house in the mornings to help her with the children. He loved his grandchildren and loved the opportunity to spend time with them and bless them.

In addition, this helped my sister to have time to get ready and do other things. Sometimes encouragement and support can be so simple.

Proverbs 3:27. Withhold not good from them to whom it is due, when it is in the power of thine hand to do it.

LIFE LESSONS

- When God lays it on your heart to do something for someone else just do it.
- Don't ask why. Don't say to yourself they don't need it.
- God told you for a reason. Just obey.
- He knows better than we do the reason why.
- Let God use you and let God be glorified.
- Find ways to "Be A Blessing".
- Do something for someone else.

How Can I Help?

1._____

2._____

3._____

4._____

Make a List of 12

Take time to make a list of 12 people that you will encourage this week. A card, a call, prayer, email... I'm sure that's not too many. Then find 12 people to encourage. No excuses. We can all find at least one person to encourage.

A sermon our Pastor preached on discipleship really took hold of me and changed my life. It took us to another level in ministry. He told us to make a list of 12 people who we would encourage and pray for on a continuous basis.

As a result of those actions the Lord blessed us with some good friendships and experiences. Some of those people are still in touch with us today even though we have moved far away.
Go forth & be a blessing. When you bless someone else you are blessed yourself!

Proverbs 18:24
A man that hath friends must shew himself friendly:
and there is a friend that sticks closer than a brother.

Hebrews 10:24
And let us consider one another in order to stir up love and good works,

Proverbs 24:17
Iron sharpens iron; so a man sharpens the countenance of his friend.

LIFE LESSONS

- Who have you encouraged today?
- Who have you prayed for today?
- Who have you helped today?
- Who have you told the good news to today?
- Who will you spend time with today?

Who are your 12 people?

As we have therefore opportunity,

let us do good unto all *men,*

especially unto them who are

of the household of faith.

Galatians 6:10

1._____

2._____

3._____

4._____

5._____

6._____

7._____

8._____

9._____

10._____

11._____

12._____

Chapter 3

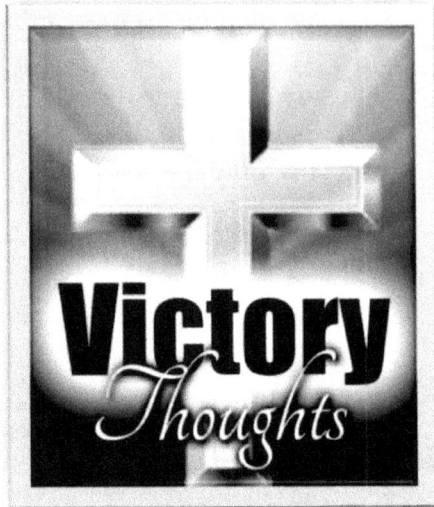

Growth, Life Lessons & Wisdom

Yes, we live, we grow, we make mistakes, we learn and hopefully we gain wisdom from that knowledge.

Moving On!!!

Can you remember a time in your life when you said to yourself – "I am moving ahead, and I am not going to look back".

I remember when I was first trying to learn how to ride a bike. My friend was teaching me. I did fine when riding straight but then I had to navigate the turn. I fell on the grate where the water goes on the side of the street. My hands were bruised and my knees where bloody. I had crosshatches in my knees where the steel cut my knees up. My friend went with me in the house and my mother cleaned me up and bandaged my knees. I was hurt. I felt embarrassed. I cried. I got over it and we went back outside and she continued to show me how to ride.

There have been times in my life that I have had to use these same principles to encourage myself to get back up again. To forget the past and start all over again. Whatever your trying moment, you have to make a decision to get up from your point of failure and move on.

Whatever your situation may be, there comes a time when you tell yourself I am going to live my life with fervor and passion. I won't accept less than God's best for my life no matter what. I will do whatever I have to do to get to the place God wants me to be. I'm moving on in victory. I will no longer live in poverty and defeat. I will not settle for defeat. I will not settle for less than God's best for my life! We may not understand it, no one else may understand it but if God is leading us we will make the necessary changes in life to move on.

A bad choice doesn't make you a bad person. There are plenty of good people who have made bad choices. You have to recognize where you are, where you want to be, and take the necessary steps to get there. Don't linger or wallow in a state or place God has told you to move from. When God tells you something to do, it is not always easy to do but it will be well worth it.

Others may try to convince you to stay. They don't understand. It's something you have to do for you. When making decisions the final decision is always between you and God. You will be accountable to God.

Philippians 3:13-14

Brethren, I count not myself to have apprehended:
but this one thing I do, forgetting those things which are behind, and
reaching forth unto those things which are before, I press toward the
mark for the prize of the high calling of God in Christ Jesus.

LIFE LESSONS

- God has more in store for you!
- You'll will never receive it unless you let go of the hurt'
- Move ahead to the bright & exciting future God has in store.
- Walk in faith! Not fear!
- See yourself blessed and walking in victory.
- Spiritual, emotional and physical blessings.

I Will Move Forward

1._____

2._____

3._____

4._____

5._____

6._____

7._____

8._____

Our Testimony

Never be ashamed of what you have gone through. It's a part of your testimony. We don't get too specific with the details of our lives but those who know us know that we have been through a lot. Some things we would hope that no one else would have to experience.

Some people wish an experience never would have happened. We just thank God He brought us through and continues to bring us through. If we had not gone thru the hardship, the tears, the anxiety, the fears, the heartache, the suffering we wouldn't be the strong praying man and woman of God that we are today.

Our prayer life and relationship with God became stronger and deeper. We learned to pray until we got a breakthrough. We watched as God changed things in our lives. God will bless you and spread a table before you even in the presence of your enemies for His name sake. If you let Him God will get the glory out of your life. We love, live and speak Romans 8:28 over our lives daily. ALL THINGS are working together for our good. God's going to get the glory out of this!

Matthew 5:16
Let your light so shine before men, that they may see your good works, and glorify your Father which is in heaven.

I Peter 2:12
Having your conversation honest among the Gentiles: that, whereas they speak against you as evildoers, they may by your good works, which they shall behold, glorify God in the day of visitation.

LIFE LESSONS

- Our worship and our praise is for real!
- We know God for ourselves.
- No one can change that!!!
- When you go thru something and God brings you out you come out stronger and wiser than before.
- You are building your spiritual muscles.

Not Cheap Just Thrifty

When I was about a teenager or preteen my mother was sick and couldn't do her usual household jobs. We each received assignments to pick up the slack and help to keep the household running smoothly.

My mother taught my sister how to cook. She would prepare dinner. My assignment was to go to the grocery store and shop for the food for the family.

My mother gave us a list and off we went. Once we were at the store my father told me to find half the items and he would find the other half.

I went down one aisle and found everything on my list. Excited I saw my father come down the aisle and I said, "Look what I found Daddy! Everything is here!" That was the day we were introduced to the "No Frills" Aisle. My Dad loved it. My father would always say if it's the right price then buy 2. If it was clothing then buy one in every color. That was my Dad.

We came home and I couldn't wait to tell everyone! My mother asked did we get everything on the list. I said yes and I have some change for you too. She couldn't believe it. She was delighted, to say the least.

The food was the same it just came in plain white boxes with big black letters. We put the food away someone commented that I was cheap. My Dad chimed in and took up for me. He said, Vivian is not cheap. She's just thrifty. **Read John 6:1-14**.

LIFE LESSONS

- Know how to save & stretch a dollar.
- That's what I call a blessing.

God Our Provider

I remember a day when I came home from shopping and just stood in the kitchen saying, "Thank You Jesus. Thank You Jesus." My son walked in the room and asked what was wrong. I explained that I was overjoyed because before I left the house the cabinets were empty and now they were full and overflowing.

My daughter walked in the kitchen and asked my son what was wrong. He explained to her what was happening. I started talking about how God will provide.

It was an Aha moment for me. I felt like my mother. Now I know why she would praise God for what seemed like the littlest things. Yes, I'm becoming like my mother and that's a good thing.

Many years later I am saying to my husband that it seems the blessings of God are overtaking us. God has provided for us in so many ways. He has given us favor. He has given us wisdom and direction to obtain the things we need. Yes, God Will Provide!

Read Deuteronomy 28:1-14

LIFE LESSONS

- Do you take time to stop and thank God for the little things?
- If you haven't, you should!!!

Thank You Lord for Providing

1._____

2._____

3._____

4._____

Still Learning

God is always using my eight year old son to teach me something. Yesterday when I was working I asked my husband to fix me a salad. He brought it to me and then I came out of the office and said, "My Chicken Nuggets are cold!" Then my little one turns to me and says "Mom, my milk is cold!!!" I looked at him and said, "It's supposed to be cold." I got the point.

Children live what they learn. Yes, they do. Lord, help us to pick up on the gentle reminders to get ourselves in check.

Lord, help us to be thankful and Lord, help us to repent when necessary.

'Out of the mouth of babes and nursing infants
You have perfected praise'.
Matthew 21:16

LIFE LESSONS

- Life teaches us lessons and finds us tests.
- Will we learn from what we have experienced or will we miss the point of the lesson and have to try again?
- You're never too old to learn something new.

What Have I Learned?

1._____

2._____

3._____

4._____

Have You Ever???

Have you ever been lonely? Have you ever been alone? Have you ever been discouraged? Have you ever been rejected? Have you ever been homeless? Have you ever needed a friend?

Have you ever been down to your last dime? Have you ever felt bankrupt? Have you ever felt cast aside?

Has Jesus picked you up? Has he made a way? Has he brought you out? Has he turned your life around? Has he put a praise on your lips and joy in your heart?

Thank You Lord that because you live within my heart you have made me new! You have delivered me from all those self -defeating predictions and negativity that tried to swallow me up and keep me from fulfilling my destiny.

Imagine what you could do if you trusted God with all the pieces of your life!!! Have you ever seen a person rise again from the ashes of defeat? If you haven't you can! Look in the mirror and thank God for bringing you out! Thank God for making you all you can be. Thank God, Thank God, Thank God for VICTORY!!!

. 2 Corinthians 5:17
Therefore, if anyone *is* in Christ, *he is* a new creation; old things have passed away; behold, all things have become new

LIFE LESSONS

- Dare to dream.
- Open your heart, mind and soul to the possibilities God can do in you and through you.
- Decide to cast all you cares upon the Lord.
- Decide to lift your hands in praise to the Lord.
- What would life be like if you trusted God completely, totally and with your whole heart?

You Win Some, You Lose Some

Growing up my uncle and I would always play one game after the other. Checkers, Monopoly, Backgammon and more. We would play, play and play again. We kept score from one game to another. My father also would play checkers with me. I would tell him – "I don't want you to let me win, I want to figure out how to win for myself." They encouraged the winner in me.

One day I was teaching my nephew how to play checkers while my father watched. He said – "Let him win". I said "No". So he named himself as my nephew's advisor and showed him how to win the game.

Our house is full of games. Our children love to see me get excited. Whenever I win I go crazy. "Oh yeah, uh huh, I am the winner." Yes! Sometimes I'd even do a little dance! Yeah I really get into it!

My husband rarely plays games with me. A little while ago we decided to play air hockey. My God why did I even ask him to play? I lost terribly. He enjoyed every moment of it. I could only imagine him thinking – "Yeah, I'm the man." He hit the puck so fast I never even saw it fly by. We laughed so hard until we cried. The rolling on the floor type of laughter. I loved it. A woman likes it when a man shows his strengths. At least I do.

My husband and children are good at math. Really good. There is a game we play called – "Mancala". I showed my children how to play after that 9 out of 10 times they would beat me. A humbling experience. LOL.

Read Proverbs 3

LIFE LESSONS

- Learn how to be a graceful winner
- Learn how to be a graceful loser.
- It may take time and effort but it's worth it.

Be Strong & Fear Not

I remember recently when I had to go in the hospital for testing and then surgery. It was the third time I was having this procedure. Once I was in the operating room the doctor told me at the last minute, that the procedure would be a little different this time and for precautionary reasons he wanted to put me on a machine to help me breathe until he completed the procedure.

I was alone in that operating room with just doctors and nurses. No one from my family was allowed in there for me to ask if I should or shouldn't do this. Half awake and half groggy I gave my permission and signed the papers.

I lay there praying, saying Lord, my life is in your hands. Thank God it all went well. I did have to have surgery later BUT GOD brought me through. Thank You Jesus!!! I will not be afraid.

Deuteronomy 31:6
Be strong and of a good courage, fear not, nor be afraid: for the LORD thy God, he it is that doth go with thee; he will not fail thee, nor forsake thee.

LIFE LESSONS
- You have to know Jesus for yourself.
- You have to know how to pray for yourself.
- You have to believe and trust God for yourself.
- One day you will be all alone and you need to know how to call on Jesus for yourself.

Chapter 4

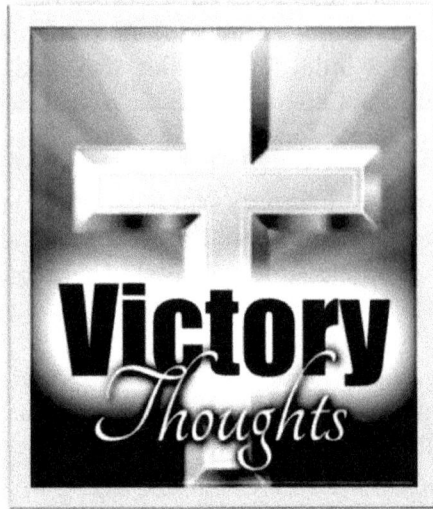

Love, Marriage
& Family

True love and marriage are a lifetime commitment.
They include sacrifice as well as passion and pleasure.
The love of Family is one of life's greatest joys.

He Found Me!

Life and love can leave you hurt and broken. However, GOD CAN redirect your life and make you whole no matter what you have been through. You have to believe that!

I decided to do as the Bible says- I would delight myself in the Lord and He would give me the desires of my heart.

> Whoso findeth a wife findeth a good thing,
> and obtaineth favour of the LORD.
> **Proverbs 18:22**

The Bible says – He that findeth a wife findeth a good thing. I refused to go looking or to "Put myself on the market." I just delighted myself in the Lord. I served Him, I worshipped Him, and I praised Him with my whole heart!

I lived many years alone focused on career and ministry. I was not looking to be in a relationship. I was totally focused on the Lord and completing the assignment he placed on my heart. I kept myself busy. I didn't have time to think about being alone or lonely.

My life was full and I was happy. BUT GOD had other ideas in mind for me. He wanted me to be complete.

One summer during the "Youth for Christ Crusade" I along with two others did the devotional for the week. One of the young people stopped participating and sat in the audience. That left myself and this new church member leading the worship alone.

I really didn't pay much attention to him. I did notice that he could really pray up a storm. He had a joyful spirit. He knew how to call on Jesus. He was filled with the Holy Spirit. He loved the Lord with the same passion and enthusiasm as I did.

Why weren't the bells ringing for me? I never thought of being involved in a relationship. It really was all about Jesus and ministry for me.

One Sunday while singing a solo I noticed him looking at me, laughing and talking to his friend. I ignored him and kept singing. He tried talking to me and it went right over my head because my mindset wasn't on a relationship. My friend told me I think he likes you. I said no, no that's not it. I think he's having some issues in one of the church groups he's in and wants to talk about it. Ok, call me blind.

One Sunday as I was folding the bulletins in the back of the church he leaned over from the back pew and said "Good Morning Sis. Vivian." I replied "Good morning Bro. Moses".

This time something made me take a second look. His hair was cut and he had on a nice suit. Yes, he was looking good! Much different than before. I think I saw fireworks! LOL. God took the scales off my eyes and I saw him in another light. I was a bit flustered to say the least but I felt good about it.

We began to pray together, talk and share. There were many things that came into play to discourage, stop, block and hinder us. Most of our dates centered on church and going out to eat. We kept it quiet and didn't let others know we were dating. I called him "Brother Moses and he called me Sister Vivian".

He proposed. I accepted. God blessed us to become husband and wife. God has been blessing us ever since. Learning and growing together in the Lord while building our family.

LIFE LESSONS

- Don't rush. Trust God for the right person.
- Your true love may be right in front of your eyes and you don't even recognize it.
- Seek God and Stay prayed up.

Godly Priorities

We've had our good days, our challenging days and our great days. In the midst of it all we are committed to hang in there together. I love my husband with all my heart and I know he loves me as well.

The main components of our marriage is that we both have a relationship with the Lord and we are both filled with the Holy Spirit.

Growing up one of my friends would say you want to be with someone who loves the Lord like you love the Lord. You can be saved but still unequally yoked if you're not on the same page as to how much you love the Lord and serve Him.

When we first got married we had a time my husband would wake up early in the mornings and pray in the spirit. Loudly. I tried to explain that he was waking others in the house. We finally got on the same page. Every day he does his "Prayer Walks" through the house.

There are many times the Lord will wake one of us up early in the morning to pray or to write. We have an understanding that when God is dealing with us we let him do so.
The Lord has given us wisdom and understanding over the years. We continue to learn and grow together. Our marriage is Christ centered.

Marriage *is* honorable among all, and the bed undefiled.
Hebrews 13:4

LIFE LESSONS

- Are you equally yoked???
- Are you on the same page with your hopes, goals, and your dreams? Are you heading in the same direction?
- Do you both love the Lord with the same intensity and passion? Do you see the person as part of your destiny?

Living, Loving & Laughing

When we first got married we went to an amusement park. I longed to be with my husband and please him so I stepped in the car, strapped myself in and went for a roller coaster ride.

My husband had a ball! He laughed so hard he cried. Everyone around me laughed too! They were laughing at me!!! I was yelling, I was screaming, I was enjoying the ride but scared.

We were in the front on the roller coaster which made it worse. I saw all the steep hills and dips before everyone else. I held on tight as my body was jerked and whipped from corner to corner. I was yelling –"Never again! I only did this because I love you!"

I was laughing hysterically when we finally stopped. I needed help getting out and I stood still for a while until I was steady. I looked at my husband and daughter and all they could say was – "Let's go on the ride that goes upside down." Of course I sat that one out.

Sometimes we do things for love that we would never imagine doing otherwise. Lord, help us to love you and live for you. Help us to chase after you Lord and long to please you.

Read 1 Corinthians 13

LIFE LESSONS

- How far will you go to please the one you love?
- How far will you go to be obedient to the Lord?

Partners in Prayer

Growing up I would hear my dad ask my mom to pray for him. None of us knew that he was sick. Not even sure if he knew but he knew he wasn't at his best. Yet you could see him growing in prayer, and his relationship with God and others daily. One thing my husband and I love about our relationship is that we are Partners in Prayer. We also have a few people who we can really go to and share with when we need prayer and we appreciate that. We are Prayer Partners. I appreciate the fact that I can roll over and wake up by my honey. Tell him I had a bad dream and ask for prayer. I appreciate the fact that I can tell him I'm having a hard day or I'm tired and I need him to pray me through. I appreciate the fact that we have cried together over situations, prayed together and believed God for BREAKTHROUGHS!!! He prays for me and I pray for him. We watch as God works in our midst. We are able to share our hurts and concerns and it works for us. We talk, we listen and we pray. Prayer is one of the skills we use to enhance our relationship. Prayer draws us closer to the Lord and to each other. When something goes wrong and we need space we can take a little break. Go to the store, go in the room to watch TV, do something else but pray separately and trust God to fix it so everything is ok when we come back together.

Do two walk together unless they have agreed to do so? **Amos 3:3**

Two are better than one, because they have a good return for their labor: If either of them falls down, one can help the other up. But pity anyone who fall sand has no one to help them up.

Also, if two lie down together, they will keep warm. But how can one keep warm alone? Though one may be overpowered, two can defend themselves. A cord of three strands is not quickly broken.
Eccl. 4:9-12

LIFE LESSONS

- Marriage takes a lot of work and commitment.
- Even when you are Partners in Prayer it takes work.
- Building a prayer relationship has to be something you do "On Purpose".

Prayer & Intercession for Families

Praying for God to bless and keep families together and growing strong in the Lord. Praying for families to have vision and purpose. Praying for heads of households. Praying for husbands and praying for wives. Praying for love and respect to abide in the household. Praying for strong relationships. Fill our hearts and minds and homes with your word Lord.

Praying for families to set Christ like examples in the home. Praying for salvation for parents and children. Praying for the Holy Spirit to move in the hearts of unsaved and backslidden family members. Praying for conviction and direction in Jesus name. Bind the hand of the enemy who seeks to kill, steal and destroy. Lord, you came to give us life and life more abundantly. John 10:10. Help, us to resist the devil so he will flee from our   families.

Praying for children that their purpose and destiny willed be fulfilled in Christ. Praying that the enemy will not rob of children of their innocence and their purpose. Praying that the word of God will come back to their remembrance and cause them to be who they should be in Christ.

Lord, give us a hunger and thirst for righteousness. A hunger and thirst to do right, to live right, to walk right. Order our steps Lord. Put your hedge of protection around our children Lord in the name of Jesus. Let them use their gifts, talents and abilities for your glory Lord! Open their eyes that they may see. Don't let them be drawn in and deceived by the tricks of the enemy. Put your word and your thoughts in their mind this day Lord. Turn their hearts toward you. Put people in their lives who will speak your word and remind them of who they are in Christ.

Be glorified in our hearts and in our homes. In Jesus name we pray. We thank you and praise you Lord in advance. In Jesus name. Amen.

Make a Prayer List

Who is the Lord bringing to your mind and
placing on your heart to pray for today???

Stop and take time to pray for them now.
Keep them in mind to pray for them daily.

1._____

2._____

3._____

4._____

5._____

6._____

7._____

8._____

9._____

10._____

My Husband
(The Worshipper)

Changing the atmosphere. I took my nap and about to get ready for work. My husband was doing his walk thru the house singing and praying. He was singing - "Hallelujah to the Lamb, I am the Great I am". We spontaneously had family prayer. I asked our little one to say thank you Jesus. He yelled out "Thank You Jesussss!!! We finished and I sat down to check my computer. All of a sudden I start singing and praising God. Singing - "Hallelujah to the Lamb..."

Read Psalm 34

LIFE LESSONS

- Prayer and worship can be caught as well as taught. It can change the atmosphere.
- That's why it's important who we hang out with.
- Just like you catch a cold you can catch another persons' spirit.
- Make sure you are placing yourself in the right atmosphere to receive what you want in your life.

Why Be a Worshipper?

1._____

2._____

3._____

4._____

Overcoming Anger

My parents believed in having pre-marital counseling before performing a wedding. Many times they would do the sessions together as husband and wife. They would say to everyone right now you are in the lovee, dovee stage but what is important is how you will handle your anger. How will you react when you disagree?

You have to go into the relationship with the proper perspective. You must understand that there will be disagreements and there will be misunderstandings. How will you handle them? There are two distinct personalities coming together. You have to learn how to mesh, blend, how to disagree without tearing one another apart. How to listen and how to communicate effectively so you walk away with understanding and resolutions not hurt feelings.

I remember a Pastor teaching a class we were enrolled in. He shared that his wife said she packed her bags and was going to leave him. He in turn packed his bag and said ok, where are we going? He said if you're leaving I'm going with you. I learned from that, that there are many days you may feel like packing up and leaving but if you have made the choice to be in it together. You do what you have to do, to work it out.

Keeping in mind that a man must know how to love and respect his wife. He should love her and care for her as Christ loved the church and gave himself for her. Sacrificial love.
You are to wrap her in your arms and hold her tight. Calm her worries and fears. Provide for her. Protect her. Never harm her physically, mentally, emotionally, or spiritually. Do not speak down to her or belittle her in any way.

A woman in turn must show love and respect to her husband. Don't speak down to him and belittle him. Don't take his pride and crush his heart like a paper ball in your hands.

Be angry and do not sin. Don't let the sun go down on your anger,
neither give place to the devil.
Ephesians 4:26-27

Husbands, love your wives, even as Christ also loved the church, and gave himself for it; That he might sanctify and cleanse it with the washing of water by the word, That he might present it to himself a glorious church, not having spot, or wrinkle, or any such thing;
but that it should be holy and without blemish.
Ephesians 5:25-27

LIFE LESSONS

- A successful marriage involves each party caring for the things that pleases his/her partner.
- A successful marriage needs two people who know how to say, "I'm Sorry" and "Forgive Me" many times...
- A successful marriage needs two people who forget the "Bad Days" and focus on the "Good Days".
- Learn to never go to bed angry.
- Don't hold grudges.
- Do what you have to – build trust and keep it. Value it, appreciate it and preserve it.
- When God brings you together you are one.
- When you love your husband or wife you are loving yourself!!!

How Will Let Go of Anger?

1._____

2._____

3._____

4._____

Priorities

When I have to make a choice I always prioritize by what's important to me. Some days I feel like super woman. Others days I need just a little more Jesus and a little more sleep. LOL. My priorities have changed and that's ok because I am changing, growing, living and loving my life every day.

I heard someone say – "I can have it all". May be you can but in my world in order to make it all work I have to prioritize. Time for God, time for me, time for hubby, time for my son, time for work, time for ministry.

If I go over in one area it will affect another area. In my life I have to start my day alone with the Lord, otherwise I become frazzled and out of sorts. Time to get myself together. Then I can handle everything else. In the midst of my busy day I always make sure to take a nap so I'm fresh for work. I have found if I don't do these things for myself I am the one who suffers. That's when my son looks at me and says – "What's the matter with you?" LOL. Prioritize.

As Jesus and his disciples were on their way, he came to a village where a woman named Martha opened her home to him. She had a sister called Mary, who sat at the Lord's feet listening to what he said. But Martha was distracted by all the preparations that had to be made. She came to him and asked, "Lord, don't you care that my sister has left me to do the work by myself? Tell her to help me!"

"Martha, Martha," the Lord answered, "You are worried and upset about many things, but few things are needed—or indeed only one.[f] Mary has chosen what is better, and it will not be taken away from her."
Luke 10:38-42

LIFE LESSONS

- My priorities are my relationship with God.
- My marriage/family, work and ministry.
- I have learned to be me and accept and love myself.

Hearts Full of Love

When you love, that love produces more love. You love your parents, you love your brothers and sisters, you love your spouse, you love your children, you love your grandchildren, you love your friends, you love your enemies, you love those who have poured into your life, your mentors and those you develop relationships with, not only at home, but school, job, ministry and more.

Through ministry you share God's love with others as you share yourself. Your capacity to love is not limited. Being the daughter of a Pastor and Pastor's wife I saw my parents reach out to tons of people. They shared their time, resources and their hearts. Sometimes they were accepted and sometimes they were hurt but they continued to love. There were always people around.

In time I learned more about ministry and serving. The importance of opening your heart to others. The importance of not being selfish. This was their passion. They were following God's will for their lives. My parents taught us that family is more than blood relatives. It's the people he put in your heart, in your life to share.

Read 2 Kings 2:1-14

LIFE LESSONS

- People are in your life for a reason or for a season.
- It is God's will for our lives to touch other lives, to share Christ, to motivate and inspire others.
- Our lives were never boring.
- We benefited from seeing Christ love modeled for us in our daily lives.
- Family, Church Family, Extended Family are all a blessing.
- There is enough room in our hearts for all of them.

A Family Created By God

At our wedding, a comment was made that we both came from rich heritages. That was a way of saying we came from two different worlds. Man looks on the outside but God looks on the inside.

God knows our hearts and he knows what he is doing. We just have to listen to him and trust him. God is truly amazing.

My husband's prayer life has developed out of the life he has lived and his experiences. My prayer life as well has developed out of the life I have lived and my experiences.

My husband came from a little island called "Jamaica." He grew up in a large family with plenty of brothers and sisters.

I came from an island too, Long Island, New York. I had one sister and one brother but plenty of cousins and extended family.

My husband grew up in the city of Kingston, Jamaica. A place of beauty, strength and pride. He experienced all of the positives and negatives of city life. He had to overcome many traumatic experiences and memories.

My husband had to adapt to his surroundings in order to survive. His wounds go deep but God has healed many of them. Yet there are things you never forget.

I grew up in Roosevelt, New York. A town that was one square mile. Mostly middle class families at that time. Mostly African American families working hard and trying to make a better life for themselves and their children. A small town but filled with love, strength and proud to be a "Rough Rider."

Only God can take two people from two different backgrounds and blend them into one heart and one mind. God reached across the ocean and brought my husband here, then he let him find me and he brought us together. That's amazing!!!

We are not perfect but we do our best and leave the rest to God. From day one of our marriage our oldest daughter was with us. She was a part of the ceremony. When I married Moses Sr. I married her. I gained an immediate family.

A few years later we brought the other children from Jamaica to the United States. We looked at this as an opportunity to share and bless someone else.

We worked, prayed, served God and made many sacrifices to have the best experience for our children.

Vivian was the only one in our household that wasn't from Jamaica. Thank God she is a tough God fearing, praying, Holy Ghost filled woman. We've had good days and not so good days. We never regret any of them.

We love our children with all our heart and nobody better not mess with our children. Our children make our family a complete family.

After almost ten years of marriage, rearing four children together, God blessed us with our youngest son. His brothers and sisters love him. We call him MoMo (aka Moses Jr.) God has used this little boy to knit our family closer together.

I used to have a refrigerator magnet that said – "God made us a family." It always reminded me of the special way God brought us together.

The Lord watches over the foreigner and sustains
the fatherless and the widow, -
Psalm 146:9

LIFE LESSONS

- When you trust God your life may be different but it will always be blessed.
- We each have situations that affect our lives differently.
- There are many different combinations to the traditional family.
- Never allow anyone to let you feel that you are less than because you come from a blended family.

Married Oneness

Marriage is about two whole people coming together to share their hopes dreams and goals. They believe that life together will be greater than life apart. In the marriage covenant and in the marriage bed the two become one. Marriage is not about your 50% and my 50% coming together. It's about each of us giving 100%. Giving our all to make it work.

In our household we do whatever we have to do to make things work. We both cook, clean, wash clothes, run errands, food shop, spend time with our son we are Team Johnson.

Every relationship is different but there has to be a point where the two become one. Otherwise you are just two people living under the same roof. Living separate lives with separate goals and no direction. One person is not making all the sacrifices while the other is living it up! We communicate until we get it right. We have agreed not to look for a way out but to let Christ in. Christ is the head. It may have been said before but it pays to say it again, Christ in our lives makes the difference in our marriage.

We are not perfect. We annoy each other and get on one another's nerves at times. We ask the Lord to teach us how to love, forgive, understand and how to be a better mate. Most of all we love another and are committed to one another and the success of our marriage covenant relationship. Every day is a new opportunity for success. We put one another first. We fall down at times but we get back up again, learn from our mistakes and do better the next time. Yes, we are at that point when one starts a sentence and the other finishes it. LOL. We are one.

Read Ephesians 5:21-31

LIFE LESSONS

- In marriage it's no longer I but it is WE.
- It's no longer about ME, ME, ME but it's about US.
- It's not about yours and mine. It's about OURS.

Responsible Fathers

My husband became a father at a young age. His mother told him that he had to step up, be a man and take care of his responsibility. He did odd jobs, worked to help provide for his children while going to school. He did the best he could with what he had. It's rare nowadays for a father to take his children and rear them. I do know of many who have done so. Some parents help each other and split the time with the child.

My mother used to say you need more than a man who is going to give you some diapers and a box of milk. We need true fathers who care and will spend time with their children.

As I am writing this my son is out with my husband. Nothing fancy just some "Daddy and Me" time. My son was on the computer and had a fit because he didn't want to get off the computer to go with dad. I took that moment to share a life lesson. I explained that mom and dad love you and when you don't want to spend time with us it hurts our feelings. He closed up the computer and was up and out the door to spend time alone with dad. A relationship is a two way street. Fathers have to reach out but the children must accept the attempt to draw closer and the love being shown. It is important for fathers to take the time to pour into the lives of their children.

Life can get messy. There are a lot of imperfect situations BUT GOD can turn it around and get a message out of it for his glory, when you give your life to him. If you are a young parent or a single parent, for whatever reason you have to tell yourself "I can make it and "I will make it."

Read Proverbs 7:1-4

LIFE LESSONS

- Thank God for our Heavenly Father.
- God wants our earthly fathers to step up and do what he created them to do.
- No excuses. It's your job to love, care and provide.
- Work on building and fixing relationships.

Celebrating Dads

When Father's Day comes I always want to make it a memorable day for my husband. We do special things for him, making cards, giving gifts and cooking or taking him out to eat. Little things just to let him know how much we love him and appreciate him. We love to read the texts, Facebook messages and take phone calls just to hear, "Hello, I love you, Happy Father's Day." There always comes a point in the day when we remember our fathers. God blessed us both to have fathers and fathers-in-love.

My Dad was always there for our family growing up. When my father died and my mother remarried years later we appreciated the love and relationship with our Father-in-Love. Even though we were grown it was important to have a father speak into our lives.

Like many, my husband's father wasn't in the home. However, when his mom found love again he had a Father-in-Love who he called "Daddy". Mr. Wilbert Stewart was placed by God in the home to be a father and blessing to him. He helped to train him as a young man. As we discussed this book my husband shared about his friends' father from Jamaica. His two friends' names were Marcus and Barry and their father's name was "Mr. George." He said Mr. George would gather up his sons' friends, take them crabbing, fishing, and teach them how to play sports and have fun. He said Mr. George took the time to pour into the lives of other young boys who didn't have their fathers around. Thank God for people like that. People who take the time to care. A father to the fatherless-**Psalm 68:5**;

Though my father and mother forsake me, the Lord will receive me –
Psalm 27:10'

LIFE LESSONS

- If you have a father in your home "Thank God" for him. Fathers need love too.
- Love him and appreciate him.
- If you want a relationship with your father then reach out.
- If you are unable to do that God will be your Heavenly Father and give you all you need.

Time to Laugh

One thing that is constant in our home is laughter. My husband loves to laugh. His laughter is contagious. Our youngest son has gained his dads laughter and then some. He will laugh and laugh and laugh.

I have found if it's one of those days and I'm feeling kind of down I turn on the TV to something funny. It takes my mind off of me and lifts my spirit. Thank God for laughter! How often do you laugh?

Growing up my father would always tell us stories to entertain us. He loved to share stories and illustrations in his sermons to help you understand better. He loved a good laugh. My mom would buy him those books with good Christian jokes as well.

I definitely inherited the art of storytelling and telling jokes from my father. It started out as a coping mechanism. I went through so much that I decided to laugh not cry. I made a change in my attitude to focus on the positive and try my best to find something to smile about each day.

A cheerful heart is good medicine, but a crushed spirit dries up the bones.
Proverbs 17:22

LIFE LESSONS

- Laughter is always good medicine.
- Nowadays many churches even invite Christian comedians because they see the value in laughter.
- Stop for a moment. Lighten up and take time to laugh!

What Makes You Laugh?

1._____

2._____

Family Time!

Some people love Basketball, Some love Football, at my house it's SOCCER. Relaxing and enjoying "Family Time". Soccer, Westerns, The Cosby Show, Computer Games, Animal Crackers and lots of Laughter. Life is what you make it. The best part of "Family Time" is just being together.

I love watching my husband watch a soccer match. He is normally pretty quiet but when he preaches the Word of God or when he watches soccer matches, he comes alive. He will yell, scream and shout GOAL!!!!!!! He talks at the TV and yells at the players and the referee.

> Do you not know that those who run in a race all run,
> but one receives the prize?
> Run in such a way that you may obtain it.
> **1 Corinthians 9:24.**

LIFE LESSONS

- What makes you come to life?
- What excites you?
- What are you passionate about in life?
- Love your family.
- Spend time, be kind & serve one another.
- Make no room for regrets. Tomorrow is not promised.

I Will Make Time for Family

1._____

2._____

3._____

4._____

Family Legacy

Today as we shared in family time we talked about leadership and how the Jews in Genesis told their children about their heritage.

We took the time to tell our son about how his parents grew up, his sibling, aunts and uncles. We told him about his grandparents on both sides.
We have a big plastic box with programs, journals, pictures and information to share with our son about his family when he gets a little older. We want him to know that he has a great family legacy.

We told him about the importance of having a relationship with God. We let him ask questions and we answered. Then we taught him how to lead us in prayer.

Tell ye your children of it, and let your children tell their children, and their children another generation.
Joel 1:3

LIFE LESSONS

- Who are your parents?
- Who are your Grandparents?
- Who are your God Parents?
- What did they teach you?
- What did they share with you?
- What legacy did they leave you?

Family Values

Train up a child in the way he should go, And when he is old he will not depart from it. **Proverbs 22:6**

I thank God for my family. I grew up in a close knit family. My father had five brothers and one sister. I grew up with lots of cousins on both sides of my family. Lots of uncles and aunts on both sides of the family.

My great grandfather was a preacher, my grandfather was a pastor, and he would tell us stories of how he built the church from the ground up with his sons and some others helping him. Years later right out of college my father became the pastor of the church followed by my brother.

For many years the brothers and their families would get together for Thanksgiving with our grandparents. It was one long table and a multitude of children.

We use to get together and sing as a family. My Uncle Rev. Larry Mackey wrote a song for us – "Here, Here Come the Mackey's, "Here, Here Come the Mackey's, "Here, Here Come the Mackey's, Singing Zion's Songs." Lord, help me to teach my children the importance of family.

LIFE LESSONS

- We were taught that God came first in our lives and then family.
- "Love God, Live for God, Serve God and Help Others.
- Family is everything.
- Stick together. Pray for one another. Help one another.
- Don't give up on one another. Be proud of who you are."

Godly Examples

That you may tell your children and grandchildren how I dealt harshly with the Egyptians and how I performed my signs among them, and that you may know that I am the LORD." **Exodus 10:2**

Lord, let our children see that we trust you daily. That's why we tell our children, God did it, we're waiting on God, God made a way, when God blesses us, and God blessed us.

We want them to know it is God who we are trusting and believing. That helps them to go to God in prayer on their own behalf.

LIFE LESSONS

- Our parents taught us how to pray by example.
- Pray about everything and in the midst of everything.
- Praise God in the good times, the not so good times.
- Pray and praise while waiting on the Lord.
- Instill within your child the importance of prayer.

Steps I Will Take

1._____

2._____

3._____

4._____

Time with Our Munchkin

It's ranging between 92 and 95 degrees every day.
With the humidity it's feeling like 100.
It's sunny in the morning and storms in the afternoon/evening.
Trying to find something to keep our little one busy inside.

Today has been a pretty busy day. Breakfast, church, dinner, go for a walk, go to the store, TV time, play some ball, computer time, drawing, arts and crafts, trying to get him to play air hockey with me. No one wants to play air hockey anymore. LOL I took a nap. Dad took a nap. Meanwhile he's wide awake and full of energy.

Lord, help us to make the most of the opportunities to spend time with our children.

My son, hear the instruction of your father,
And do not forsake the law of your mother;
for they will be a graceful ornament on your head,
And chains about your neck.
Proverbs 1:8-9

LIFE LESSONS

- We love spending time with our little one.
- Thank You Lord for strength!
- Taking time to play a game he made up.
- Sing, dance and make up songs.
- Even though we're getting tired we know this day will never come again.
- Make special memories.

Looking Good Baby!

My son doesn't like to get his hair cut. I love to keep it low and shaped up so you can see the waves in it. He gives his father a hard time whenever he tries to cut his hair. He yells, screams, sometimes cries, complains and then finally lets him cut it.

Today he came in the room after getting his hair cut and I said – "Baby you look so handsome." He immediately ran out the room to his father and told him – "Mom said I look handsome." He had a big grin on his face. He was glad he had his hair cut.

I laughed to myself and thought how we are like that. We don't want to experience the trials and hardships we have to go through to get our blessing. We lack patience. We whine, mourn, complain and throw a fit. Then we finally give in and say- "Ok Lord whatever you want!" Once we receive the blessing we are happy, and joyous, thanking and praising God.

We glory in tribulations, knowing that tribulation produces perseverance; & perseverance, character; & character, hope.
Romans 5:3-4 NKJV

LIFE LESSONS

- God wants us to grow and mature.
- God wants us to know that He's working for our good.
- God wants us to trust him immediately. Totally.
- God wants us to no longer be spiritual babes.
- God wants us to be rooted and grounded in him.
- Wow. All of that out of a haircut. LOL. God is good.

Teachable Moments

I remember one day when my daughter and I were making dessert. We were making a chocolate cake for dinner. When we took the cake out of the oven the middle sunk in. I had to think quickly.

I had learned a lot from mother and her baking cakes for the church. We let the cake cool then we filled the middle with cut up bananas. We then put the cake on a plate flipped it over and put on the icing.

My son came in the kitchen and asked what we were making. I looked at my daughter and said, "It's a chocolate banana upside down cake."

Then I told her never tell anyone what you're cooking just in case you make a mistake you can call it something else. LOL. All that mattered was it tasted great.

LIFE LESSONS

- Be open to change.
- We learn from our mistakes.
- We can always begin again.

What Can I Share?

1._____

2._____

3._____

4._____

Stir Up the Gift within You

My mother would always say – "You need a skill to fall back on." Our first Christmas as a family we purchased a computer for our oldest daughter. She took typing class and eventually she began to help out at church by typing the midweek programs. She loves working with children and works with early childhood education.

When our children were growing up God allowed us to see some of their talents and special skills. Both of our sons love to draw, they are artistic, creative and talented. One of our daughters loves to do hair and fashion. She also loved to bake. Our other daughter loved to be creative, write poetry and sing.

Our youngest son has a big desk in his room. Every day he sits at his desk and draws, writes and makes what he calls arts & crafts. He makes what his teacher calls 3D art. When he's bored with that he goes on his computer to read and play games. He's been taking computer classes since Pre-K.

He is a little computer whiz. He loves the computer. At seven he knows basic computer language and a few advanced skills. We want to help him develop that talent. We are creating an atmosphere for growth. We are helping him to stir up his gifts.

*Wherefore I put thee in remembrance that thou stir up the gift of God,
which is in thee by the putting on of my hands.*
II Timothy 2:16.

LIFE LESSONS

- We all have special gifts and talents within.
- Has God placed something within you but it is lying stagnant and dormant in your life?
- What are you doing to stir up your gift?
- Believe in yourself and the gift which God has placed within you to make a difference.

What Are Your Natural Talents & Abilities?

List how you can use those talents for the glory of God.

1._____

2._____

3._____

4._____

5._____

6._____

7._____

Teaching Our Children

One day we heard our son talking to himself out loud in the hallway. He evidently was thinking something thru. He finished talking and didn't realize we were listening to every word. Vivian was in her office behind the closed door. She heard him and answered his question out loud. He started saying "Thank You God. Thank You God."

We tried explaining to him that it was Mommy but he insisted that he heard God speak to him. He said I couldn't see him but I could hear him. We found it to be a good opportunity to teach him about God and faith.

He went on to say "Mom I know you believe in Jesus and Dad believes in Jesus. Now I believe in Jesus. I know He is real." He said, "I know he's real because I can feel him in my heart." He was so excited and happy. What a blessing to know Jesus for yourself.

Jesus answered and said unto him, "Verily, verily, I say unto thee, except a man be born again, he cannot see the kingdom of God."

John 3:3

LIFE LESSONS

- Lord, help our child to always be open to hearing from you.

- Lord, help us to know your voice.

- Help us to believe with child-like faith.

Teaching Our Child to Pray

The other day I was praying over my grocery list. I went to look in the freezer and it was nearly empty. Just a bag of chicken nuggets and some vegetables left. I stood there looking at the bottom.

I was seriously praying about God stretching my funds. As I stood there looking at the empty freezer my son walked up. Spontaneously I told him to lay his hands on the freezer and repeat after me. We said, "Father God in the name of Jesus please fill up this freezer with food. In Jesus name. Amen.

The next day I took him to the school bus and then I went food shopping. I never quite had an experience like this. To me it was a miracle! The previous month I had spent the same amount but this month I had more than double.

I walked thru the aisles praying and picking up the items on my list. My basket was full and I went to the cashier. Once she totaled everything up I realized I had a lot of money left. I went to the car and put the food I purchased in the trunk. At that point I realized that I forgot something. So I went back in the store.

When I went in the store in my spirit I heard, "Check the chicken". Previously I didn't but any chicken because it wasn't on sale. I had called my husband while shopping and told him chicken was on sale across town and could he pick it up for me. He told me to just go ahead and buy it at the store I was at. However, I didn't purchase it on the first go round because the price was too high.

I listened to my spirit and immediately went to the meat section. There was a gentleman in a white coat and I asked him if there was any chicken on sale. He said, "Just a moment. I'm reducing the prices right now." You can only imagine my excitement. About fifteen minutes before the same meat was full price. I waited patiently as he put the stickers on and reduced the price. I filled my basket. I went on to pick up a few other items and went to cash out once again. I paid for my items and still had money left. Wow!!!!

I went home and my husband helped me to put the food away. The freezer was full to the brim. Once again I realized I forgot something else and went back to the store. (Thank God I live right near the store). I proceeded to pick up the items I forgot previously.

Then my mind said go to the dollar store. I went and purchased items and filled my cart. When I came home and put the food away not only was the freezer full but the pantry was full too and the fridge partially full.

Three baskets of food. When I normally get one for just a bit more than I paid the previous month! That's God. Now my baby can see that God does answer prayer.

> Therefore I say unto you, what things soever ye desire, when ye pray, believe that ye receive them, and ye shall have them.
> **Mark 11:24**

Read John 6:1-14
It tells how God used a little boy's fish and loaves to feed five thousand. God is in the business of multiplying.

> But my God shall supply all your need according to his riches in glory by Christ Jesus.
> **Philippians 4:19.**

LIFE LESSONS

- Pray before you shop and while you shop.

- Ask God to lead you and guide you.

- Pray over your purchases and ask God for wisdom.

- Pray in faith. Believing.

- Tell your children how God answers prayer.

Building on the Rock

The other day we were in the car driving and our son starts telling a story. He said- "You know some people build their house on sand and some people build their house with bricks and some people build their house with sticks. It is ok if you want to make your house out of sticks, but if you do, you have to make sure you have a firmmmmmmmmmmmm foundation." We burst into laughter. "Have you been reading the three little pigs?" "No" he said - "I've been watching Veggie Tales". He said it in his little preacheristic voice. It wasn't exact but we knew the idea came from the word.

Matthew 7:24-25
Therefore whosoever hears these sayings of mine, and doeth them, I will liken him unto a wise man, which built his house upon a rock: And the rain descended, and the floods came, and the winds blew, and beat upon that house; and it fell not: for it was founded upon a rock.

LIFE LESSONS

- Lord, help us to expose our children to your Word more and more on a daily basis.

- Help our children to hide your word in their hearts.

- Lord, help us to build upon a firm foundation. Jesus Christ our rock.

Scriptures to Memorize

1._____

2._____

3._____

4._____

Something Awesome!!!

Our son says last week - "Let's do something awesome." We told him to get his ball and let's go outside. We went outside and played kick ball until we worked up a good sweat and then went for a short walk. (It was about 95 degrees outside).

We finished playing and were ready to go inside when he said - "Was that supposed to be awesome?" The answer was "Yes it was!" He said - "Oh, Ok". It was 95 degrees outside. Of course that was awesome!!!"

The following Friday we told our son – "Today is an Awesome Day". We ran a few errands in the morning then we went to the library for Movie Day, but it was Scientist Day and they had an Animal Show. Spiders, lizards, alligators and a big gigantic snake to name a few. The kids loved it. Our son had mixed emotions. He played on the computer a bit, then off to get some Dr. Seuss books and videos. Awesome Day is about spending time together and doing things he finds enjoyable.

Our son had a shirt that he loved to wear. It said, "This Kid is Awesome." It even glowed in the dark. We walked around the house saying in our WWE Wrestling voices, "This Kid is Awesome!!!!!!!!" It was our way of motivating him and helping him feel good about himself.

But Jesus called them to *Him* and said, "Let the little children come to Me, and do not forbid them; for of such is the kingdom of God. Assuredly, I say to you, whoever does not receive the kingdom of God as a little child will by no means enter it."
Luke 18:16-17

LIFE LESSONS

- Lord, help us to remember to show love to one another daily and to find ways to let our children know they are AWESOME!!!

A Never Ending Love

Being a parent is one of the most joyous experiences in the world. However it can be a joy and a challenge as you watch your child grow and go thru the different developmental stages. Walking, talking, and running, climbing everything is exciting during those first few years. Then they begin to grow and wonder, asking questions. What is that? Why? Why? Why? Then they learn to say NO! What a time, what a time, what a time! They build the blocks then throw the blocks. LOL.

We have to watch them fall and learn to get back up again on their own. Still it's a time to enjoy because the teen years are coming!

During the teen years they love you, they hate you, they need their privacy and on and on. One day you're their best friend, the next day you're their worst enemy. LOL. Funny when you look back but not when you're going through it.

The young adult years they want their independence. They want to stretch, grow and do what they want do. Parents are old fashioned and out of touch with what's happening. They know better. They know everything. It's my life. Leave me alone.

You are tested and tried. Those are the years of many prayers. We have to learn to let go even though we want to hold them tight and show them the way.

During those years my mother would always say – "Keep the lines of communication open. There's never anything you can't tell me." We have all been there in one way or another. Parenting isn't always easy but you never give up on your child no matter what they are going through.

They get their first car. A good job. Get established. May be married with children. Then it starts. What am I doing with my life? Where am I going? What have I accomplished? Do I enjoy what I am doing? I want more out of life.

Once you have it down pat and feel you are making progress you soon realize – "My parents are getting older, I need to spend more time with them, I need to let them know how much I love them and care". You look for ways to share and care. If you are blessed you become friends. This is when they want their parents in their lives.

Can you say – WOW! Lord, thank you for parents who have hung in there with their children through all the stages in life. Help us to listen, learn and appreciate the wisdom of our parents. Help us to recognize their never ending love.

> Behold, children *are* a heritage from the LORD,
> The fruit of the womb *is* a reward.
> Like arrows in the hand of a warrior,
> So *are* the children of one's youth.
> Happy *is* the man who has his quiver full of them; they shall not be
> ashamed, But shall speak with their enemies in the gate.
> **Psalm 127:3-5**

How Can I Show Love?

1._____

2._____

3._____

4._____

5._____

6._____

7._____

Time with Your Parents

Whenever my mom comes to my home to spend time I am like a little child. I look forward to just being with her and spending time together talking, sharing a cup of tea or going out and running errands. My mom is my shopping buddy, and we can shop until we almost drop. Years before I got married and my father was alive I would take my mother to run her errands while my father was at work. I worked nights and was able to spend most days helping her out.

As a wife, mother and grandma myself I don't always have the same amount of time daily. However, I make an effort to speak to my mother quite often on the phone. Sometimes it might just be to check on her or to give some encouragement. Sometimes it's to share some facts or ask for prayer for a particular situation.

I work with seniors daily, talking to them and sharing information. Sometimes people just need to hear a friendly voice or know that someone cares. Unless we leave here early we will all become a senior one day. Bless your parents.

Exodus 20:12
Honour thy father and thy mother: that thy days may be long upon the land which the LORD thy God giveth thee.

LIFE LESSONS
- Lord, help us to treat our parents with the love, respect and care that they deserve.
- Help us to appreciate our parents.
- Help us to listen as they share their wisdom and stories.
- Help us to learn all we can from them.
- Do what you can to bless your parents.
- Time goes so quickly. Don't let a day go by .

Rejoicing & Weeping

Rejoice with them that do rejoice, and weep with them that weep.
Romans 12:15

I remember vividly how excited certain family members and friends were for us when we completed our first book. Their words of encouragement were a blessing to us. It only takes a moment to say a kind word to someone else.

In our immediate family we were taught to rejoice with others. I remember when my twin nephews were born. We waited downstairs in the lobby and as soon as we go the word we all ran to the phones to say the news with family and friends.
Even though I didn't have any children of my own at the time I rejoiced when every one of my nieces and nephews were born just like they were my own.

The Bible says - "Rejoice with those who rejoice and weep with those who weep". Have you ever had a loved one to die and you hear someone say – "I going by the house to sit with the family for a little while." They would bring a cake or fry up some chicken and take it to the house. They would give them a card with some money tucked in it, they would pray, hug, sit a while and leave.

The same applies to when someone is sick and you are going to visit.

Growing up when my mother went back to school for Pastoral counseling. I would read her books after she finished them. A great book for all who are in leadership is – "What to say when you don't know what to say". I am a firm believer in leadership training.

The point was to take time to let others know you care. To acknowledge their pain and grief. (But be brief) Unless they want you to stay longer. Show them love but give them time and space.

As Christians many times we are in denial. Yes, Jesus heals, Yes they are with the Lord. Yes, God will work it for my good. However, right now I'm hurting. I don't want to hear anything. Grieving is a process. Let me weep before I move on.

When you lose someone special in your life you move forward but you never forget. We both have parents who are gone to be with the Lord. In writing this book we shared many memories and stories with one another. We cried, we laughed and we remembered together. Sharing helps to bring healing and wholeness.

LIFE LESSONS

- We miss out on our blessing when we don't rejoice with others.
- Allow people time to go thru the grieving process. Whether it is a death, a broken relationship, job loss or some other loss. Allow people time to weep, to heal and recover.
- Healing doesn't always happen overnight.

Who Can I Minister to Today?

1._____

2._____

3._____

4._____

5._____

6._____

7._____

Faith & Finances

A year before we married I was driving a white Dodge Spirit. In my back window I had a bumper sticker that said - "Angels watching over me".

It was a snowy Sunday morning. I was on my way to the church office to run off the bulletins. I came to the stop sign and all of a sudden I saw a flash of white light. I was blinded and just felt myself going forward thru the sign. Next I saw a truck flash by me. I spun around, hit a pole and the air bag exploded. I jumped out the car in a daze in the middle of the street. God is good. I hit one of those big town dump trucks. I was ok. My hands were burnt from the air bag. Later the aches and pains started but overall no broken bones. Thank you Jesus!!! The car was totaled and it wasn't covered under my policy. It sat in my driveway for a year. I struggled, working and paying 2 car notes and my mortgage.

When we married my husband had his own car. Now we had 3 cars, a mortgage and a family. I watched each month as my husband paid our tithes never missing a month. He paid the car payments and the bills. He eventually (in a short time) paid the gap amount on the car. He made a deal with an auto body shop to take his old car and repair the wrecked car. Then he traded in the Dodge Spirit and bought a new car from a dealer some years later. That was nobody but God! Over the years I have seen my husband been faithful through many situations. God always blessed us, provided for us and made a way for us with a family of six. No matter what, be faithful in your giving to God. He will bless you!!!

Without faith it is impossible to please Him, for he who comes to God must believe that He is, and that He is a rewarder of those who diligently seek Him. **Hebrews 11:6**

LIFE LESSONS

- Teach us Lord to save.
- Teach us how to stick to our budget.
- Teach us how to make wise choices.
- Teach us not to give up.

God's Favor in Finances

I remember having the desire to have my own home. I was about thirty, single with a good job and good pay I really didn't share my dream with many people because I didn't want to get discouraged. I did go to look at some new town homes that were being built and that got me started. The dream started welling up inside me.

Timing is everything! One day I came home there was a letter in the mail. It informed me that I had paid off a loan and they never cashed the check. It has been misplaced and they just found it about 6 months later. I prayed about it and felt led to get the money. After picking up the check and cashing it I went to see my mother. While I was at my mother's home, my sister called and told me news about a house. All the pieces fell into place. I was made aware of a new homebuyer program that I would have to put very little down. The money I received paid for my closing costs.

I just started a new position at my job and had enough income to qualify for the mortgage. It was a miracle and a blessing all the way around!!! God is good. Within a few months I bought a three bedroom home and my sister bought a new home too. When I bought the home I was alone with three bedrooms. A few years later after marrying and having children it was just right. Eventually we moved to a bigger home. The house came first and then the family. God knew what he was doing. Trust and believe God for what you want. He knows how to make things work together for your good! Keep trusting God!!!

"And you shall remember the LORD your God, for *it is* He who gives you power to get wealth that He may establish His covenant which He swore to your fathers, as *it is* this day.
Deut. 8:18

LIFE LESSONS

- God will work on your behalf.
- God will work a miracle for you if you need one.
- God will look ahead and provide for your future needs.

Our Creative Home

For many years I would decorate the basement of the church whenever we had special events. Bulletin Boards, color coordinate the tables, napkins, flowers, etc... I truly enjoyed serving in this way.

When God blessed us with a home of our own I transferred those skills into being a creative homemaker. I have found that I love color. I love to decorate and express myself in unique ways. I love to create a cozy and inviting atmosphere for my family and guests in our home.

My home is unique to say the least. I have created original wall art in each room. I have motivational plaques spread around the house so wherever you go there is something to minister to you. I'm not your cookie cutter type of woman.

I have found who I am in Christ and as a woman, I have filled the corners with plants and lovely picture frames with family photos. It has taken time. It didn't all happen at once but it's to a place now that I enjoy my home. It's relaxing, inviting, inspiring, it reflects me.

We love the holidays. It gives us the opportunity to share our home and our joy of giving. My husband loves to put up the Christmas tree right after Thanksgiving. He wants the feeling of Christmas to last just a little bit longer. He fills our home with Christmas music and walks around the house singing full of joy. I think it's his favorite holiday.

I remember our first Christmas with all the children. I stood behind the wall with the camera waiting to see their surprise. Each one had stacks of presents piled high. I shopped until I dropped that Christmas. I wanted each one to feel special and loved. That was my way of showing love.

Recently the Lord opened a door for us and blessed us to buy our own home once again after years of renting. The process has started all over again. Creating, designing and making our house into a home for our family.

My little children, let us not love in word or in tongue,
but in deed and in truth.
1 John 3:18.

LIFE LESSONS

- Lord, help us to find what we enjoy and do it with all our might for your glory!
- God Uses The Gift of Decorating.
- Find ways to minister to your family.
- Make your home a haven. A place of rest.
- Let your children know it is God who provides for you.
- Make your home a happy and inviting place to be.

How Can Be Creative?

1._____

2._____

3._____

4._____

5._____

6._____

7._____

Moving? Again Lord?

"Get out of your country, from your family and from your father's house, to a land that I will show you. I will make you a great nation; I will bless you and make your name great; and you shall be a blessing. I will bless those who bless you, and I will curse him who curses you; and in you all the families of the earth shall be blessed." - **Genesis 12:1-3 NKJV**

Moving is hard work. We have moved many times since we were first married. It was always to make life better for our children. Better schools, better neighborhood, and more opportunities for them... God told us to make several big moves which we did in obedience. It's amazing because God would deal with us separately, then we would come together and talk only to realize he was placing the same dream in each of our hearts. We received tremendous blessings from being obedient.

We owned our home in New York, we sold our home, we moved to a smaller apartment in the best school district with amenities. Then we moved to a bigger apartment home in obedience. Years later we moved to Pennsylvania to a lovely home with everything we wanted with a great school district, our miracle son was born there. As the older children began moving on their own we moved to a smaller apartment.

One day God spoke to us. Everything fell into place like dominoes and in obedience we moved to Florida. First we were in 2 rooms, then we moved to a 4 bedroom apartment home. We believe God will bless us for everything we gave up in being obedience.

It is here in Florida that we got the name for our ministry "Share Some Love House of Prayer Evangelistic ministries" which started as a home Bible Study in New York in the year 2000. It is here that God spoke to our hearts and we are completing our second book. You never know why God is leading you. You may not see the whole picture but it pays to be obedient to the Lord.

One thing I know for certain is that God has a plan for our lives and that his plans are for our good and will bring him glory.

Whenever I start feeling down or the enemy tries to plant doubt or discouragement in my thoughts I encourage myself with **Jeremiah 29:11**.

> For I know the thoughts that I think toward you, saith the LORD, thoughts of peace, and not of evil, to give you an expected end.
> **Jeremiah 29:11.**

LIFE LESSONS

- Lord, you may be speaking to someone's heart today about change. Help them not to be afraid.
- Help them to trust you in the midst of change.
- Help them to seek your will for their life wherever that may be.
- Help them to know the blessing of walking in obedience to you father.
- God is able to do more than we could ever think, ask, hope or imagine in our lives.
- I used to be upset that my life wasn't simple like everyone else. Then God made me aware of the privilege of being unique.

Blessing from Being Obedient

1._____

2._____

3._____

4._____

5._____

6._____

7._____

Chapter 5

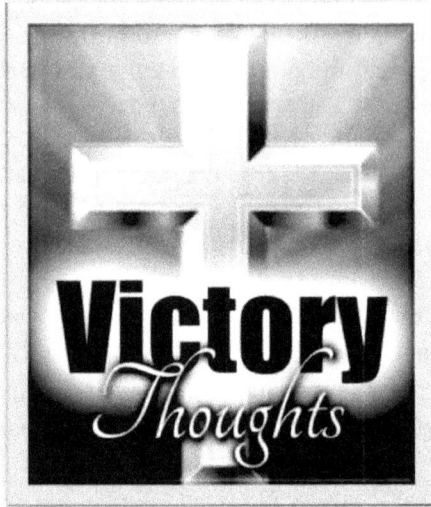

Leadership & Ministry

Becoming a leader is an act of obedience to God.
A leader is one who has a desire to serve.
Jesus is our greatest example of leadership.
Leaders are followers of Christ.

Prepare for Excellence

It doesn't matter whether you are someone looking to start a business, a ministry, buy a home or just someone who wants to better your life, you need to prepare yourself. Many say, "Do your best and God will do the rest". In many cases that is true. However, it also comes to the point of saying, "What is our best?"

First, whatever we do we should do it as unto the Lord.
And whatsoever ye do in word or deed, do all in the name of the Lord Jesus, giving thanks to God and the Father by him.
Colossians 3:17

Secondly, we should always have a spirit of excellence. I remember many years ago our church theme was, "Called to Excellence". God calls us not to be ordinary but "Extraordinary." However, it is God's spirit anointing our work which helps it to stand out. When the Lord is on your side he can give you extraordinary favor and miracles to bring your project to completion. You may fall and make mistakes but keep trying and give it your all. Don't give up!!!

Excellence has many meanings

1) Excellence is a talent or quality which is unusually good and so surpasses ordinary **standards**. It is also used as a standard of **performance** as measured e.g. through **economic indicators**.

2) Excellence is a continuously moving target that can be pursued through actions of integrity, being frontrunner in terms of products / services provided that are reliable and safe for the intended users, meeting all obligations and continuously learning and improving in all spheres to pursue the moving target. – Wikipedia.

In leadership training classes we were taught we are to give God our all. Give God our very best. We are not to half step (as my father would say) but to give God our very best offering. Leaders teach by example. We cannot lead others down the path if we ourselves have not been there before.

In the process of reaching forth and pressing toward the mark there are some questions we should ask ourselves. Here are some to get you started.

Philippians 14:13-15
Brethren, I count not myself to have apprehended:
but this one thing I do, forgetting those things which are behind, and reaching forth unto those things which are before, I press toward the mark for the prize of the high calling of God in Christ Jesus. Let us therefore, as many as be perfect, be thus minded: and if in anything ye be otherwise minded, God shall reveal even this unto you.

Always seek God in prayer for direction first. Never give God less than your best? We always Pray, Plan, Prepare and then Proceed.

LIFE LESSONS

- What is God speaking to your heart?
- Have you prayed about it?
- Have you asked God for direction?
- Are you keeping good records and notes?
- What are your hopes, goals & dreams?
- What area do you need victory and deliverance in?
- What are you doing to save toward your dream?
- Do you have a business plan?
- Have you researched your project?
- Read books. Search the internet.
- Do you know who you are looking to reach?
- What steps have you taken so far?
- Have you documented your steps?
- Have you put your vision in writing?
- What sacrifices will you have to make?
- Are you preparing yourself?

I See You in the Mirror

I remember one day shortly after my father passed I looked in the mirror and said – Wow, I look like my father! Then I looked at my hands and said Oh God I have my father's hands!

Since that time there have been many occasions that I realize I am acting like someone else who poured into my life.

One day I had a situation going on and I just started walking around the house praying and interceding with a fierce passion. When I finished I said to my husband I felt my sister's spirit all over me when I did that.

As I get older I start thanking and praising God daily for little things and for everything. Well that spirit certainly comes from my mother. She is a prayer warrior and worshipper indeed. Sometimes it's scary.

My husband spent many long hours with my father as his driver and assistant before he became ill. My father used the opportunity to pour into this young man who later became my husband.

There are many days when I see my husband do something, say something or react to something and I see and feel my father's spirit of leadership. I have even seen my husband respond like my brother who was our Pastor for several years.

You imitate and become what you are around. Watch who you spend your time with.

LIFE LESSONS

- Have you ever realized that you pick up things from the people who surround you?
- Who are you hanging out with?
- Who is pouring into your life?
- What lasting impression are they leaving upon you?

Do You Have a Mentor?

The personal name Mentor has been adopted in **English** as a term meaning someone who imparts wisdom to and shares knowledge with a less experienced colleague.

We are blessed to have various mentors at different points in our lives. Our parents were mentors for us constantly. We had many opportunities to listen and learn.

When we officially started in ministry our Mentor/Pastor was Rev. Arthur L. Mackey, Jr. (Vivian's brother). He started Pastoring at what some people may consider a young age but he started his relationship with the Lord at a young age as well. Preaching and teaching Bible Study at 13 years of age. Growing up in the church getting wisdom and knowledge that only comes from experience.

Sitting under his Pastor (our father), listening, learning, gaining valuable wisdom, knowledge, lessons, strength and understanding. He has just completed his 11th book. We are happy to follow in his footsteps as an authors, Praise God!!!!

LIFE LESSONS

- Lord, you may be speaking. God puts people in our lives to help us along the way so we can get to where He wants us to be.
- Who is showing you the way to go???
- Who is your example in life?
- Whose pattern are you following?
- Who is sharing their wisdom and knowledge with you?

What's Your Passion?

What makes you shine? What gives you joy and delight? What would you do even if you didn't get paid for doing it?

Over time I have found myself. I have discovered the passions God has placed within me.

I love Color, creativity, anything artistic, I love to write and communicate. These are some of my passions. I could stay up all night just being creative. That passion led me to become a Pre-Press Journeyman (Graphic designer) for 19 years. I have over 35 years of experience training, learning, speaking, teaching, creating, assisting, developing, organizing, implementing, leading, mentoring and helping to bring the vision of others to pass. It all didn't happen at once. I was faithful and consistent to the job at hand whether big or small.

Whether it was lemonade, cupcakes or selling hats. I loved setting goals, reaching goals and being challenged. My experience in this area gave me the opportunity to serve as a church trustee. This position calls not only that you can count and have a financial expertise but you're trustworthy. Working in the church, it is also necessary to be Christ-like and patient.

Ministering as a Church Trustee gave me a lot of experience that I can translate into the real world. I was blessed to have my uncle and others who shared their knowledge with me and taught me. It was on the job training.

So many times we miss out in life because we think we know it all. It is important to be open to learning from others. When we make a mistake it is important to acknowledge it and learn and move on.

I started reading books on finance and investing. I desired not just to do well but to excel in my knowledge of finance. My passion led me to go back to school. One of my friends who was our church organist and owned his own business encouraged me to become a life insurance agent. I worked hard and learned a lot. Those experiences prepared me for my job today as a Senior Licensed Sales Advocate.

Reaching souls for Christ in creative ways. I love to teach. Sharing with people, I enjoy hearing good preaching but I really love to teach and evangelize. God used many people in my life to teach me and train me in ministry. I thank God for the many Women in Ministry God used to pour into my life.

My husband catches on fire when he preaches the Word of God. He is also a dynamic Bible Study Teacher. You can see the love and passion in his eyes, in his movements and in his voice. He can take one sentence from the Bible and get a whole sermon out of it. He will give you scriptures and cross references then come back to the main subject and tie it up in a neat package for you to understand. Yes, he is passionate about preaching the Word of God.

It is important that we find and pursue our passion in life. There are many miserable people in life because they have not found their passion. Find your passion and allow God to use you in that particular area. It could be full time, part time or volunteer. Find a place where you can use your skills and glorify God.

Till I come, give attention to reading, to exhortation, to doctrine. Do not neglect the gift that is in you, which was given to you by prophecy with the laying on of the hands of the eldership.
1 Timothy 4:13-14

LIFE LESSONS

- What do you love to do so much that you would volunteer your time to do it?
- What makes you so excited that you will stay up all night just to make sure it's right?

Redesign Yourself

My mother would sew and make our clothes. She would bake bread and cakes. She would clip coupons and shop the sales. As the saying goes she knew how to make ends meet. I believe that is a trait she truly passed on to me which helped me through some tight times.

I watched as my mother translated her family skills into ministry skills. I saw my mother put on her jean outfit and run the food feeding program during the summer at the church. I saw her complete reports, stay in her budget and manage a staff. I saw her serve as the Missionary President, Vacation Bible School Director, organize the Prayer Partners, do Outreach Ministry, the Single Parent's Ministry and so much more. I saw my mother reach out to the Ministers' Wives and Widows. I saw her love God, love people, reach out to people and share from the depths of her heart and resources.

I watched my mother recreate herself after all her children were grown. She went back to school and received her degree in Pastoral Counseling. She began her counseling ministry.

I saw her growth. She evolved into a strong Christian Woman. Beautiful on the inside as well as the outside. It was like watching a butterfly spread its wings and fly.

My mother is much more than a woman in fine clothes and a beautiful hat. She knows how to network, coordinate, organize and is a top notched administrator. A praying woman, full of the Holy Spirit, a **Proverbs 31** woman.

LIFE LESSONS

- Lord, teach us how to be all that you want us to be.
- Help us to know there is more inside of us.
- Teach us Lord to be accepting of where we are in life.
- Teach us how to redesign ourselves if necessary.

Protecting Your Dream

Sometimes it's better to keep quiet about what God is speaking to you and what God is doing in your life. Many times God starts moving in our midst bringing the vision to pass so we can run to tell everybody. It's natural to be excited and want to share, but sometimes you have to wait.

This makes me think of when we were expecting our son. We went thru ten years of marriage and lost three babies. Each time the pregnancy would start out fine but then something would happen and we were disappointed again.

The emergency room doctor told us Vivian was miscarrying. He told us we probably would lose the child over the weekend. Tuesday came and we went to the regular ob/gyn doctor. We looked at the sonogram and saw a heartbeat. We asked the doctor is that the baby? He said yes and everything was perfectly fine.

We agreed to keep it quiet and not tell everyone. Vivian went to the high risk clinic and stuck to her diet. She did exactly as she was told. Each month my faith would get stronger seeing my belly grow. We talked to the baby, sang to the baby and prayed over the baby. At about six months one day we agreed to tell everyone. Good thing we did at about seven months her belly popped out and we could no longer hide it.

While waiting for my husband to arrive the nurse had me push but nothing was happening. The nurse checked me out and found that my son's head was not in the proper place because my uterus was tilted. She physically put her hands in and positioned my son's head where it should be. Soon after my husband entered the room. She told me to push again and everything started happening.

God gave us favor. My doctor and her assistant (who was a Christian) knew what I had been through before. They stayed hours after their shift and helped deliver the baby. They laughed with me, talked with me and even cried with me.

It was an exciting event. About 9pm, May 22nd, 2007. Dancing with the Stars season finale was on TV. Just as they were celebrating the winners of the finale on the TV Moses Johnson Jr. made his appearance. Our dream had come to pass. Take time to protect your dream!!! Some told us it would never happen. God sent us to a hospital in Allentown Pennsylvania where the doctor told us they specialized in delivering babies to high risk mothers. Look at God!!!!!!!!!!!!

Trust in the Lord with all your heart,
and lean not on your own understanding.
In all your ways acknowledge Him,
and He shall direct your paths.
Proverbs 3:5-6

LIFE LESSONS

- Don't believe everything people tell you.
- Always believe what God tells you.
- Exercise your faith.

Steps to Protect Your Dream

1._____

2._____

3._____

4._____

5._____

6._____

7._____

Praying for Your Pastor

If you want to be blessed and if you want your local church to be blessed you should wrap your Pastor, spouse and family up in prayer daily. When was the last time you prayed for your Pastor? When was the last time you encouraged your Pastor? When was the last time you asked God to be a blessing to your Pastor? I recently read an article online about Pastors. It detailed how many of them give up. Commit suicide. Leave the ministry. Retire. People look on the outside but they have no idea what sacrifices a true man and woman of God make to fulfill the will of God in their lives. Our Pastors, spouses and family need our prayers to undergird them and lift them up. This is serious. What a privilege to intercede for the man and woman of God.

Finally, brethren, pray for us, that the word of the Lord may run swiftly and be glorified, just as it is with you,
2 Thessalonians 3:1;

Brethren, pray for us.
1 Thessalonians 3:25; And I will give you pastors according to mine heart, which shall feed you with knowledge and understanding.
Jeremiah 3:15.

LIFE LESSONS

- As leaders our job is to lift up the hands of our Pastor and be supportive.
- Stop and think. How can you pray for your Pastor today?
- How can you pray for your Pastor's Spouse & Family?
- Encourage others to pray for the Pastor.

Be a Problem Solver

And it came to pass, when Moses held up his hand, that Israel prevailed: and when he let down his hand, Amalek prevailed. But Moses' hands were heavy; and they took a stone, and put it under him, and he sat thereon; and Aaron and Hur stayed up his hands, the one on the one side, and the other on the other side; and his hands were steady until the going down of the sun. **Exodus 17:11-12.**

In ministry there is always work to be done. Sometimes the burden gets heavy for the Pastor. Through Vision of Victory Ministries our job was to help uphold the arms of the Pastor.

There is an expression "You are known for the problems you solve." As a wife, mother and homemaker I am always finding problems and looking for solutions. I remember sitting in my living room and having Bible Study. Each time I sat down, God would show me something that needed to be done in our home. I would listen to the Lord, write down what was in my spirit and take action to move towards that goal.

One time I heard God say – "Save." I had no idea why but I shared it with my husband. We moved some things around and started to save instead of spend. The Lord started dealing with me about areas of finance in our lives. When the opportunities arose we had options because we listened and saved.

LIFE LESSONS

- God can use you to be a problem solver. In your church, in your home, on your job and over your future.

The Worship Life of a Leader

Our praise comes from the most inner part of our being. When we praise God start by thanking him for what he has done and what he is doing. As we start thanking him our praise flows into worship. We start blessing his name. Lifting our hands to receive from God, lifting our hands in thanksgiving. In the black church experience we sing, we shout and give glory to God.

God has blessed us to have a unique blend. Vivian grew up in a black Baptist Church. Traditional in some ways but evolving to more of a Baptist/Pentecostal experience. Moses grew up in Church of God in Prophecy. When we married we transitioned to more of a nondenominational experience.

We have experienced all types of worship. Lively and expressive, Quiet and reserved, Pure and contemporary Praise and Worship styles, Hardcore praise, worship and bless your name Jesus. On your knees, on your face, crying out to the Lord type of worship.

All of those experiences have helped to build and strengthen us. As leaders we should be able to worship with others who don't necessarily promote the same style of worship we are used to.

A good leader though must have a life that encompasses Prayer, Praise and Worship. You must have time alone with the Lord in your daily life.

You can't expect to have a fresh anointing in your teaching, preaching and leading if you are not spending time in God's word. This is not just for preachers but for all who serve as leaders. we are talking about a right now leadership.

Let me say here worship is not just for leaders. When we have "Praise & Worship" it is not a spectator event where the leaders worship and the congregation looks on. Corporate worship is everyone together on one accord reaching out to the Lord in our own way. The duty of the Praise & Worship Leader is to lead us into worship. It is a journey we experience together. We move from level to level as we express our love for God.

If we are God's servants. God's representatives who need to have a private prayer life. We should have practiced together in our home, thanking, praising and worshipping the Lord.

When we get in public and we are asked to lead worship or to intercede in prayer, we are prepared. We are worshippers. Our love for God flows from within us into the atmosphere as we encourage others to come bless the Lord. You can tell when someone has spent time with the Lord. You can tell.Over the years I have seen new leaders struggle as they were called on in public. You could see the struggle. As others encouraged them to press on, you could see breakthrough.

When I think of God's goodness and all he has done for me I can't help but "Praise Him". Lord I love you, Lord, I thank you, Lord, I bless your name. Lord, I exalt you. Lord, I worship you!!!!! Hallelujah God!!!! Lord, I bless your name!!!!! Thank you Jesus!!!!!

Psalm 42:2
I thirst for God, the living God. When can I come and appear before God?
(Holman Standard Christian Bible)

Matthew 5:6
Blessed are they which do hunger and thirst after righteousness:
for they shall be filled.

LIFE LESSONS

- How is your private prayer life?

- Are you exuding praise and worship?

- Are you connecting to God?

- Are you hearing from God in your time alone?

- Are you seeing a difference in your life?

- Can you see God's hand at work?

Leaders Should Be Readers

What a mighty God we serve! I have always loved books and love to read. As a young girl I would stay locked in my room for hours reading. My friends and I would walk to the library and get books each week.

God blessed me with a husband who loves books and learning as well. Today our home is filled with books we have added to our leadership library over the years. Growing up I accompanied my mom to the Christian Bookstore almost every week. My mom was the one who instilled within me a thirst for knowledge as far as books were concerned.

My dad loved books on jokes, Bible trivia, sermons and leadership. My mom loved books on Pastoral Counseling, caring, ministering to hurting people, leadership and more. What a blessing! As a Pastor and Pastor's wife I saw my parents give books as gifts and encourage the leadership to read and grow in the Lord.

We are all leaders in some way. Whether we are parents, teachers and even students. We all benefit from reading. Not only our Bible but other God inspired books as well.

Many years after those experiences my brother, Pastor Arthur L. Mackey, Jr. has authored 11 books. Most recently my husband, Elder Moses Johnson Sr. and I were inspired to write our first book – "Daily Inspiration thru God's Word". This is a devotional to encourage others in their quiet time with the Lord.

We thank God for the opportunity to write and share with others. Thanking God for anointed men and women of God, writers who have taken time to write the vision and make it plain that we may read it and run with it.

I remember when my mom was the Superintendent of the Church School she would always say – "Each one, Reach one till all is won for Christ".

For my people are destroyed for lack of knowledge...
Hosea 4:6

And the LORD answered me, and said, Write the vision,
and make *it* plain upon tables, that he may run that readeth it.
Habakkuk 2:2

Lord, bless those who write and bless those who read and run with the vision. In Jesus name. Amen.

Lord, help us to be open to reading good books but most of all help us to read and study "The Good Book" your Holy Word. The Bible.

What Books Have You Read Recently? How Have They Helped & Blessed You?

What Are You Looking Forward to Reading Soon?

1._____

2._____

3._____

4._____

5._____

6._____

7._____

8._____

Leaders Need Good Manners

It may seem like something that everyone should understand but you would be surprised at the way some leaders conduct themselves. My mother taught us to treat people the way you want to be treated. Never look down on anyone. As leaders we should be humble and friendly. We always tease my mother because she speaks and says "Hello" to everyone she meets. She has good people skills. People can recognize when you have manners and use them. I was speaking to a stranger and they told me - "Tell your mother she did a good job of home schooling you." It may seem old fashioned but good manners never go out of style. "Please, Thank You, etc..." When you work in ministry you have to be able to deal with all types of personalities. Some people are more difficult to deal with than others.

Even though our personality types may differ as Christians we should all be filled with God's spirit and exhibit the Fruit of the Spirit. That's for sure. We need the Holy Spirit active and at work in our lives to make sure we are walking in the spirit and not the flesh. We are not our own. We can't say or do anything we feel like saying or doing. We have to submit ourselves to the Lord to guard our tongue and keep our mind stayed on him at all times.

Galatians 5:22-23
But the fruit of the Spirit is love, joy, peace, forbearance, kindness, goodness, faithfulness, gentleness and self-control. Against such things there is no law.

LIFE LESSONS

- If you've made a mistake, done something wrong, hurt someone. Ask God and that person for forgiveness.
- If you want to be blessed and move ahead. It needs to be done.
- Use the Word of God as your guide and final authority.
- Remember our light should be shining for all to see.
- Leaders are expected to set good examples.
- Have an intimate relationship with the Holy Spirit so he can correct you when you are wrong.

We Need the Holy Spirit
(Biblical references for the importance of the Holy Spirit)

1. He leads and directs.

(Matt. 4:1; Mark 1:12; Luke 2:27; 4:1; Acts 8:29; Rom. 8:14)

2. The Holy Spirit speaks – in, to and through.

(Matthew 10:20; Acts 1:16; 2:4; 13:2; 28:25; Hebrews 3:7)

3. He gives power to cast out devils. (Matthew 12:28)

4. He releases power. (Luke 4:14)

5. The Holy Spirit anoints. (Luke 4:18; Acts 10:38)

6. The Holy Spirit "comes upon" or "falls on".

(Matt. 3:16; Mark 1:10; Luke 2:25; 3:22; 4:18; John 1:32-33; Acts 10:44; 11:15)

7. He baptizes and fills.

(Matthew 3:11; Mark 1:8; Luke 1:15,41,67; 3:16, 4:1; John 1:33; Acts 1:4-5; 2:4; 4:8,31; 6:3,5; 7:55; 10:47; 11:24; 13:9,52; 1 Corinthians 12:12)

8. He gives new birth. (John 3:5-8)

9. He leads into worship. (John 4:23)

10. He flows like a river from the spirit man. (John 7:38-39)

11. He ministers truth. (John 14:17; 15:26; 16:13)

12. He dwells in people. (John 14:17; Romans 8:9,11; 1 Corinthians 3:16)

13. The Holy Spirit gives comfort, health, and strength. (John 15:26; Acts 9:31)

14. He proceeds from the Father. (John 15:26)

15. He shows us things to come. (John 16:13)

16. He gives the gift of tongues. (Acts 2:4)

17. He releases prophecy, dreams and visions. (Acts 2:17-18; 11:28)

18. He can transport people physically. (Acts 8:39)

19. The Holy Spirit brings direction and guidance.

(Mark 13:36; 13:11; Acts 10:19; 11:12; 21:11; 1 Timothy 4:1

20. He is Holiness. (Romans 1:4)

21. He is the Spirit of life and gives life. (Romans 8:1-10)

22. The Holy Spirit invites us to walk with Him. (Romans 8:4-5)

23. He groans, prays and intercedes. (Romans 8:26-27)

24. He is a Sword. (Ephesians 6:17)

25. The Holy Spirit produces fruit in our lives.

(Galatians 5:22-23; Ephesians 5:9)

26. He helps us in our weakness. (Romans 8:26)

27. He bears witness.

(Acts 5:32 15:28; 20:23; Romans 8:15-16; Hebrews 10:15; 1 John 4:13; 5:6-8)

28. He is the Spirit of Adoption. (Romans 8:15)

29. He gives power to mortify the deeds of the flesh. (Romans 8:13)

30. He provides power for signs, wonders and preaching.

(Acts 1:8; 1 Corinthians 2:4)

31. He ministers love. (Romans 15:30)

32. He searches the deep things of God. (1 Corinthians 2:10)

33. He quickens the mortal body. (Romans 8:13)

34. He brings revelation.

(Luke 2:25; 1 COrinthians 2:10-12; Ephesians 1:17-19; 3:5)

35. The Holy Spirit reveals to us what has been given by God.

(1 Corinthians 2:12)

36. He washes, sanctifies, purifies and justifies.

(Romans 15;16, 1 Cor.6:11; 2 Thess.2:13; 1 Timothy 3:16; 1 Peter 1:2,22)

37. He gives gifts. (1 Corinthians 12:4-11; Hebrews 2:4)

38. He seals us. (2 Corinthians 1:22; Ephesians 4:30)

39. He is liberty. (2 Corinthians 3:17)

40. He changes us into the image of Christ. (2 Corinthians 3:17)

41. He is the promise of the blessing of Abraham. (Galatians 3:14)

42. He releases a cry to the Father. (Galatians 4:6)

43. He gives access to the Father. (Ephesians 2:18)

44. The Holy Spirit builds us together for a house for God. (Ephesians 2:22)

45. He strengthens us with might. (Ephesians 3:16)

46. He is unity. (Ephesians 4:3-4)

47. He is wine. (Ephesians 5:18)

48. He supplies. (Philippians 1:19)

49. He is fellowship. (2 Corinthians 13;14; Philippians 2:1)

50. He is grace. (Hebrews 10:29)

51. He is glory. (1 Peter 4:14)

52. The Holy Spirit speaks to the churches. (Revelation 2:11,17,29; 3:6,13,22)

53. He calls for the Bridegroom. (Revelation 22:17)

54. The Holy Spirit has the power of conception and anointing for God's purposes. (Matthew 1:18,20; Luke 1:35)

55. He teaches. (Luke 12:12; John 14:26; 1 Corinthians 2:13; 1 John 2:27)

56. He gives commandments. (Acts 1:2)

57. He provides power to be a witness. (Acts 1:8)

58. He provides boldness. (Acts 4:31)

59. He give sight. (Acts 9:17)

60. He commissions. (Acts 13:4)

61. He restrains. (Acts 16:6)

62. He appoints ministries and gives them authority. (Acts 20:28)

63. He releases love. (Romans 5:5)

64. He is righteousness, peace and joy. (Romans 14:17; 15:13; 1 Thessalonians 1:6)

65. He confesses Christ's Lordship. (1 Corinthians 12:3)

66. The Holy Spirit brings the gospel. (1 Thessalonians 1:5-6)

67. He is keeping power. (2 Timothy 1:14)

68. He brings renewal. (Titus 3:5)

69. He moves on believers. (2 Peter 1:21)

70. He convicts the world. (John 16:8)

God's Way of Doing Things

God has his own way of doing things. At times we think we have it all figured out. We can outline exactly how it should be done. Then God says "Stop" don't do it. The Lord will sometimes lead us another way than the one we have planned out.

We have to trust that HE KNOWS exactly what he is doing and why. We have to trust and believe that he has our best interest at heart.

There are times when God has spoken to my husband or vice versa and said – "Do this". It may have seemed silly or the long way of doing it but we were obedient and God blessed us.

We may never know why God does things the way he does or sometimes he allows us to look back and see the reason why. God's way is always the best way.

Never try to do God's work with your own methods. It won't work. Pray and get in tune with God. Make sure you can hear him clearly.

I Samuel 17:38-50 tells us about the story of David preparing to fight the giant Goliath. King Saul has his own idea of how he should suit up to fight. God had a different idea. Read on and be blessed.

I Samuel 17:38-50
Holman Christian Standard Bible

Then Saul had his own military clothes put on David. He put a bronze helmet on David's head and had him put on armor. David strapped his sword on over the military clothes and tried to walk, but he was not used to them. "I can't walk in these," David said to Saul, "I'm not used to them." So David took them off. Instead, he took his staff in his hand and chose five smooth stones and put them in the pouch, in his shepherd's bag. Then, with his sling in his hand, he approached the Philistine.

The Philistine came closer and closer to David, with the shield-bearer in front of him. When the Philistine looked and saw David, he despised him because he was just a youth, healthy and handsome. He said to David, "Am I a dog that you come against me with sticks?" Then he cursed

David by his gods. "Come here," the Philistine called to David, "and I'll give your flesh to the birds of the sky and the wild beasts! "

David said to the Philistine: "You come against me with a dagger, spear, and sword, but I come against you in the name of ·Yahweh of ·Hosts, the God of Israel's armies — you have defied **Him.** Today, the **LORD** will hand you over to me. Today, I'll strike you down, cut your head off, and give the corpses of the Philistine camp to the birds of the sky and the creatures of the earth. Then all the world will know that Israel has a God, and this whole assembly will know that it is not by sword or by spear that the **LORD** saves, for the battle is the **LORD**'s. He will hand you over to us."

When the Philistine started forward to attack him, David ran quickly to the battle line to meet the Philistine. David put his hand in the bag, took out a stone, slung it, and hit the Philistine on his forehead. The stone sank into his forehead, and he fell on his face to the ground. David defeated the Philistine with a sling and a stone. Even though David had no sword, he struck down the Philistine and killed him.

LIFE LESSONS

- Look at God. God is truly amazing!!!
- He already knows the answer.
- He already knows about your battle.
- He already has made a way for you!!!
- He already knows what method he will use to deliver you. Trust that He knows what He is doing.
- He already has the victory in his hands!!!!
- Praise God, Hallelujah, Thank You Jesus! Glory to God!!

R-E-S-P-E-C-T
Never Goes Out of Style

Growing up our parents taught us to never look down on anyone else, treat people the way you want to be treated and give respect and honor to whom it is due.

When I started my first full time job at the telephone company most of my supervisors were African American women. We called them by their last name- Mrs. Jones, Mrs. Thomas etc. Many years later I started working for a major newspaper. I came to work dressed up in my work clothes. Everyone else except for one person dressed casual. I had to learn this new way of doing things.

One day I was speaking to my boss and he told me to call him by his first name. I had to explain that where I came from we didn't call our elders by their first name. It took me awhile to get comfortable with it. However, I never forgot who was the boss and always made sure to give respect. In my family we have a lot of preachers and pastors. My mother taught us that whenever we were in public we were to address others according to their title/office. We were taught to give respect even though they were family members. Years later my brother is the Pastor of the church I grew up in and we always say Pastor Mackey and refer to him as Pastor. We call my cousin Bishop Mackey. It is good training. God will bless you when you respect the man and woman of God.

Bondservants, obey in all things your masters according to the flesh, not with eyeservice, as men-pleasers, but in sincerity of heart, fearing God.
Colossians 3:22

LIFE LESSONS

- Lord, help us to honor and respect the anointing you have placed upon the man and woman of God.
- Help me never to consider ordinary what you have blessed and made extraordinary.
- Help me never to disrespect or undermine the leader you God, have placed in my life.

Accountable Leaders

When we know the right thing to do but we persist in doing the wrong thing the Lord hold's us accountable.

And that servant, which knew his lord's will, and prepared not himself, neither did according to his will, shall be beaten with many stripes.
Luke 12:27

But he that knew not, and did commit things worthy of stripes, shall be beaten with few stripes. For unto whomsoever much is given, of him shall be much required: and to whom men have committed much, of him they will ask the more.
Luke 12:48

How are you accountable?
To whom are you accountable?

List ways you can be more accountable.

1._____

2._____

3._____

4._____

5._____

6._____

7._____

Excited About Ministry

May the favor of the Lord our God rest on us; establish the work of our hands for us, yes, establish the work of our hands. **Psalm 90:17.**

We are excited about what God is teaching us, showing us and revealing to us. We thank God for growth, direction and establishing the work of our hands. Yes Lord we thank you!!! We praise HIM in advance!!!!

My father used to always say – "Rescue the perishing & care for the dying." He quoted the song- "If I can help somebody then my living shall not be in vain." He lived his life in such a way to teach, to leave people better than you found them and to make a difference.

Lord, bless leaders today, encourage them, strengthen them, and build them up in the name of Jesus. Lord, help us to follow your leadership. Help us to make a difference. Positively and prayerfully. Amen.

LIFE LESSONS

- Are you blooming where you are planted?

- Are you making a difference?

- Are you touching lives for Christ?

What do you enjoy about ministry?

1._____

2._____

3._____

4._____

•

Preparation for Ministry

Looking back over our lives we can see how God prepared us for leadership in so many ways. My life was full of education and preparation for leadership. In addition to formal training God brought me through some tough times which gave me not only classroom training but life experience. I grew up in the church and in a Christian home. I wasn't prepared for a different world. I was a quiet, naïve young lady. As a result of life's experiences I took on a "Don't Mess with Me" type of attitude. I can be quiet. I can be forceful. I can be trusting. But don't misuse or abuse my trust. I learned to become a fighter and take up for myself. I believe everything I went through prepared me to be the Woman of God I am today. Physically, emotionally and spiritually I am healed. Thank God for his Holy Spirit who takes away those things in our lives that are unlike Him. Thank You Lord for helping us to walk in victory. My husband thousands of miles away had a different experience. He lived a hard life. He endured many hardships, fought to go to school and pay for his books. He was prepared on tough streets. He had to fight to survive. He had to work hard and fight for simple things which we take for granted. Then he had to fight to protect his stuff. His life lessons were live or die. Don't blink. His goal was to not become a statistic. My husband is a quiet man. Because of what he has been through he doesn't like a lot of fuss and confusion. He likes peace. He can be as mild as a lamb, but deep inside he has the strength and tenacity of a lion. There are many people who have gone through hell and back. There are many people who have experienced discouragement. There are many people who feel that because they come from a certain place they can't break free from the chains that tie them down. You can break free!!!

I Peter 1:7

That the trial of your faith, being much more precious than of gold that perishes, though it be tried with fire, might be found unto praise and honor and glory at the appearing of Jesus Christ.

I Corinthian 3:13

Every man's work shall be made manifest:
for the day shall declare it, because it shall be revealed by fire;
and the fire shall try every man's work of what sort it is.

LIFE LESSONS

- We are living testimonies that you can break free.
- You don't have to accept a life of defeat.
- You don't have to be a victim of life's experiences.
- All leaders must go through a testing process.

Name Some Ways God Prepared You for Ministry/Leadership

1._____

2._____

3._____

4._____

5._____

6._____

7._____

8._____

Visionary Leadership

As ministers and ordained elders we were assigned by our Pastor to work with the "Vision of Victory Ministries". Our job was to help fulfill the vision of the Pastor in our local church. Sometimes it might have been a big project. Other times it may have been what seemed like a small thing. Our job was to help bring the vision to pass. We were to listen to our Pastor's heart and do what was necessary to "Make It Happen".

Proverbs 29:18
Where there is no vision, the people perish:
but he that keeps the law, happy is he.

LIFE LESSONS

- Lord, bless all those who work in ministry.
- Help us to stay focused on You Lord.
- Let whatever we do be done for your glory Lord.
- What can you do to help bring your Pastor's vision to pass? How can you be a blessing to the ministry?

Are you supportive of the Pastors' vision? If so how?

1._____

2._____

3._____

4._____

5._____

6._____

7._____

Visionary Talks

God placed within our hearts to move from New York to Pennsylvania. We packed up our belongings and our three younger children and moved to the mountains of Pennsylvania.

God blessed us with a beautiful twin home at the foot of a big mountain. A small little town where they were building new housing developments.

We would wake up early in the morning and listen to the birds. We also would hear the train go by. We could see the train from the bedroom window. It was country. Deer and rabbits coming in the front yard.

It was a fresh, new experience for us. We would wake up early to see the sun coming up over the mountains. We thanked God and talked about the future. We talked about what God was doing, what God had done and what we expected God to do in our future.

We had some great times there. We also endured many challenges and hard times BUT GOD was with us all the way. We had our hands full. We were walking by faith not by sight.

The enemy will always try to stop, block, hinder or discourage you from doing God's will. During those times we quoted **John 10:10 and Romans 8:28** a lot.

God was going to bless our family with abundant life and all the not so good things that were happening, would work together for our good. Keep speaking greatness. If no one else sees it or believes it. Believe God's word.

LIFE LESSONS

- Make sure you and your spouse are on the same page.
- Take time to talk and share your dreams.
- Take time to speak life over your family.
- Always believe God for his best for yourself and your family. Walk in faith and receive God's best.

Sowing Seeds

Growing up I had a love for books. A thirst for knowledge. I lived at the Christian Bookstore. Most of the books I bought were on Christian Living and Leadership. I would give my last dollar to buy a book. I am still like that today. Amazingly my husband had the same thirst for knowledge. He too loved books. Many people today take it for granted the privilege to read. Coming from an African American background with family members who experienced slavery who couldn't read or write it takes on a new meaning to be literate. When we first married I noticed my husband loved books and learning as well. We compiled a huge collection of books. When we moved from a bigger house to a smaller one we sold much of our collection. It was hard for me because I always said my books are like my babies. We participated in a community yard sale at a local church. There was a woman who said she had a book sharing ministry. She would give books to prisoners in jail. They would read them and pass them along. God allowed us to buy hundreds of books not knowing one day they would be a seed into someone else's ministry. Somewhere in a prison in the US someone is reading one of those books. Touch Lord. Save. Heal and deliver. In Jesus name. Amen. Our dream is to one day have an expansive library in our home filled with books. Right now we are working with our son on reading. We are trying to express to him the importance of reading. Reading can open up a whole new world for you.

Ecclesiastes 11:6
In the morning sow thy seed, and in the evening withhold not thine hand: for thou knowest not whether it shall prosper, either this or that, or whether they both shall be alike good.

LIFE LESSONS
- What kind of seeds are you sowing?
- What type of ground are you planting in?
- What type of harvest are you expecting?
- Whose life or ministry are you planting into Lord?
- Are you planting into good ground?
- Help us to be faithful, consistent and help us not to be weary in well doing.

A Heart & Mind for Missions

One day I walked in the living room, the TV was on, I saw my son on the phone and he was crying. He was about nine or ten at the time. When I asked him what was he doing? He said he was calling "Feed the Children". I reminded him he didn't have any money. It stuck with me though. At that age he remembered where he came from, what he had been through and wanted to help someone else. God knew what he was doing. When it comes to missions my husband and I are on the same page. Coming from a third world country my husband has experienced homelessness, poverty, violence, bullying, and a lot more first hand.

One of our most treasured memories is working with the homeless. When we first married there was a ministry working out of the church's youth center. We helped serve dinner to the homeless on Thanksgiving and other holidays annually. What an honor and a privilege to serve. We enjoy ourselves each year and looked forward to doing it again. We both have compassionate hearts. One thing we have agreed upon is to support other ministries in giving. We feel by doing so we too are reaching and helping to meet needs. As the Lord leads us we share of our time and resources to bless others as well. Whatever we do, we do it as unto the Lord. Sometimes it may be something small, sometimes a little bit more but whatever we give, whatever we share comes from a heart of love. We receive many requests for help and don't have the funds to meet every need. We pray and believe God that there will be someone somewhere with a heart of compassion to meet the need.

> He who gives to the poor will not lack,
> But he who hides his eyes will have many curses.
> **Proverbs 28:27**

LIFE LESSONS

- The Lord blesses us so we can share with others.
- Lord, allow us to grow in our giving.
- Lord, we are your ministers. Help us to minister with a servant's heart and with compassion and kindness.

Opportunities to Serve

Growing up one thing I learned was opportunities come thru service. There are some things that need to be done in the ministry where you need a full time or part time staff. These people should be paid for their work. That is only right and fair.

In addition to paid staff there are many needs that are filled through volunteers. I have served in the church in many capacities. We started out cleaning the bathrooms, washing dishes after dinners, helping to be servers, cleaning up before service, picking up trash and bulletins, filling the water pitchers, dusting, putting away the hymnals, sweeping, mopping floors, carrying bags, carrying Bibles, picking people up, dropping people off and so much more.

I've been involved in the choir, the junior ushers, and I served as a chaplain, assistant secretary, secretary, treasurer, vice president, president and speaker. This was all by sixteen years old.

In later years I served as Part Time Church Clerk, Woman's Day Chairperson, Anniversary Chairperson (Pastor's Anniversary and Church Anniversary), Church Trustee, Praise & Worship Leader, Assistant Director of the Church School,   Coordinator of Vision of Victory, Director of the Senior Choir and the Junior Choir, Assistant to the Pastor and First Lady, and much more.

I planned programs. I typed bulletins. I created the Church Handbook for the Pastor. All of these except for the Part Time Clerk were voluntary positions. I learned many skills and gained many opportunities that people weren't giving women.

Many, many years later my calling was acknowledged and I became a minister. Later, I became an Ordained Elder. I wasn't searching for titles. I was looking to serve, I wanted to be in the Ministry of Helps. I went where I was needed and did not look for anything in return.

I must admit I did get some knocks, bruises, talked about and had some head on collisions in the process of trying to do God's work God's way. When God is on your side you learn to trust him more and more.

Help us to look and see the opportunities ahead of us. Opportunities to be a help and a blessing. Opportunities to serve.

I believe that one of the reasons God has done so much in our lives is because we followed leadership. As our Pastor followed Christ we followed him. Now if you're Pastor is not following Christ that's another issue. If your Pastor is living for God you should be following leadership.

Imitate me, just as I also imitate Christ.
1 Corinthians 11:1

LIFE LESSONS

- Lord, please bless all those who have stood and raised their hand to serve in ministry as a leader.
- Take the responsibility seriously.
- Serve the Lord and don't get caught up in the schemes.
- Seek to honor you and put the Lord first.
- The Church is not a social club, but a hospital for dying souls.

List Opportunities

1._____

2._____

3._____

4._____

Are You Running From God?

When we think of running from God we usually think of Jonah in the belly of the whale.

Jonah 1:1-3. The word of the LORD came to Jonah son of Amittai: "Get up! Go to the great city of Nineveh and preach against it, because their wickedness has confronted me." However, Jonah got up to flee to Tarshish from the LORD's presence.

Many of God's leaders have been reluctant to go forth and complete the assignment given to them. Many times we make excuses until finally we run out of these excuses and run straight into God.

When my husband told me he was going into the ministry I was surprised. Not shocked but just surprised. However I was very happy about it. I knew that he had a calling on his life from long ago.

He decided to go back into the world as a young adult for a period of time. He succumbed to peer pressure. He was persuaded to "live and enjoy life now" and serve God later. As a result he made life altering choices.

He eventually restored his relationship with God. He was running from God but realized he needed God more than ever.

I had my own experience with running from God too. I loved God and loved ministry. I was saved and I was filled with the Holy Spirit. As a teen and early young adult I was in church day and night.

I sensed God's calling on my life. In those days it was a little more difficult for a woman who was anointed and wanted to preach. I held back the urge to teach and preach. Yes, God forgive me. I quenched the spirit many, many times in order to be accepted.

In my early twenties I found fulfillment elsewhere. I became involved with people who knew God but didn't serve the Lord the same way I did. I spent many Sundays away from church. I was saved but I wasn't fulfilling my God given purpose and I knew it.

Still I had that tugging in my heart. I went to church but was just a pew member. Someone who comes to church on Sunday and warms the pew but never gets really involved.

I heard the preaching, teaching, and singing, clapped some and went home. I became a once in a while church visitor. Just enough to say I am a Christian but not enough to get immersed in the things of God. I was hiding from my anointing in the pew.

I finally started going back to church on a consistent basis. I became a vital part of the ministry. That worked great for me because I could sing, shout, dance and praise God without hesitation.

I praised God and studied the Word, and God began to deal with me more and more. God lead me to an environment which accepted women in ministry.
In spite of personal complications I remained in my new comfort zone. However, in obedience to God I decided to leave and return to my home church.

It was at my home church God opened doors for me. It wasn't easy for me. I had been away and came back home. I was welcomed with open arms.

This time though I wasn't running from God but I was running to him. I was still saved, sanctified, filled with the Holy Spirit and I didn't care who knew it. I was bold, and strong. I was an overcomer, a survivor. I had a testimony and I was focused on doing what God would have me to do.

Personally I had been through a lot. However, I survived those trying experiences and it was time to move ahead.

About twenty years after the time I felt God's calling at sixteen years old, I was licensed to preach.

You can try to run and hide from God, you can try doing something else other than what he has told you to do. However, you will never be truly happy until you are where he wants you to be and doing what he wants you to do.

> Before I formed thee in the belly I knew thee;
> and before thou camest forth out of the womb I sanctified thee,
> and I ordained thee a prophet unto the nations.
> **Jeremiah 1:5**

LIFE LESSONS

- Do you know that God has a calling on your life?
- Are you heading in the opposite direction?
- Are you in God's perfect will or his permissible will?
- Is it time to come home?
- Is it time for you to get yourself together?
- Let God use you for his glory?
- Women are Preachers, Teachers and Pastors.
- Are you on God's most wanted list?

I Will Run Back to God

1._____

2._____

3._____

4._____

5._____

6._____

7._____

Chapter 6

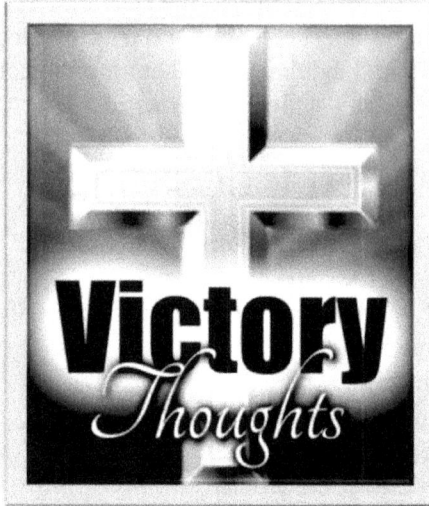

Prayer & Prayer Warriors

Prayer is simply talking to God. We pour our hearts out in prayer and we intercede for others. We long to speak to you Lord and listen to you speak to our hearts.

Getting Your Day Started

I like to BREAKFORTH in prayer. I start blessing the Lord. Thanking Him, praising Him, lifting up His name, exalting Him, magnifying Him, telling how much I love Him, thanking Him for how much He loves me and gave His life for me, thanking Him for keeping my mind in perfect peace, thanking Him for making a way out of no way, thanking Him for working miracles in our lives, thanking Him for looking beyond our faults and seeing our needs, thanking Him for saving souls and drawing souls closer to Him.

I will praise him in the car, on my job, in my home, before going to the school for a meeting, wherever I may be I stop, pray and give God thanks.

Read Psalm 34

LIFE LESSONS

- Thank You for working it in our favor Lord.
- Thank You for working behind the scenes.
- Thank You for touching hearts and minds.
- Thank You Lord.

Prayer of Praise

._____

._____

._____

._____

Stress Relieving Prayer

God is standing by waiting just to hear your cry, call him up night or day, God is just a little prayer away. God is on call 24 hours a day, 7 days a week waiting to hear from you. You can call on Jesus... Anytime, Any Place, Anywhere....

I remember when my father was in the hospital. We went to visit him one day and ran into the doctor. The doctor proceeded to load us down with a negative report. I remember the weight of that information and battling with facts, faith and fear bouncing around in my head.

I came home and sat down at the dining table feeling overwhelmed. I started to sing uplifting and encouraging songs. Songs about strength in God and how He will never leave me nor forsake me. I sang, sang and sang as tears rolled down my face. I lifted my hands in praise and started to pray. I sat there and prayed until I felt a breakthrough in my spirit. Sometimes prayer doesn't change things but it does change us.

Read acts 16:16-34

LIFE LESSONS

- Lord, you know our hearts.
- You know our needs.
- Help us to reach out to you in prayer no matter the time, place or situation.
- Prayer Relieves Stress. Try it. It works.

Stay Prayed Up

As we build our relationship with the Lord and get closer to him day by day it's natural to talk to him more and more.

Can you remember starting a relationship? Whether it was on the phone or in person you talked and talked and talked. With each conversation you learned more about each other and your relationship rose to other levels. Our communication with the Lord should be natural. It should flow freely. Prayer is not an event to be attended but it is a way of life **1 Thessalonians 5:16-18**. Rejoice always, pray without ceasing, in everything give thanks; for this is the will of God in Christ Jesus for you.

LIFE LESSONS

- When you wake up in the morning do you forget to speak to your spouse?
- Do you forget to speak to your children?
- How can we forget to talk to God in prayer?
- It starts when we open our eyes, roll over and our feet hit the floor.
- In your heart or aloud just say – "Thank You Jesus."

How Will You Stay Prayed Up?

1._____

2._____

3._____

4._____

5._____

6._____

7._____

A Praying Woman

I am a praying woman. Morning, noon and night. There are many times when the Lord wakes me up early in the morning and I can't sleep. I have to lay there and pray or I get up, go into my office and pray.

In the past few years since starting "Share Some Love House of Prayer Evangelistic Ministries" I will go on our Facebook group or page and pray with others, near and far. I love that we are able to reach others near and far away in an instant. I see it as a great ministry opportunity.

There are times when God will put someone on my mind or I will see someone's face. I don't know why but I just start praying. I pray for situations known and unknown. I pray as I post. I pray for my husband, I pray for my little one, I pray for my grown children, I pray for my grandchildren, I pray for family members, I pray for the ministry and I pray for souls to be reached and God to be glorified in our lives. I pray aloud and I pray silently. I pray in the spirit and I pray with understanding. It's my desire for prayer to flow through me and change me into a Woman of God who makes a difference and lets her light shine. Never underestimate the power and importance of a praying woman.

Read 1 Samuel 1:8-18

LIFE LESSONS

- A woman who takes time to listen to the Lord to pray and intercede for others is of great value.
- You never know how your mother's or wife's prayers are keeping you.
- Thank God for his Angels watching over us.

A Strong Praying Man

A Praying man is a unique man. He has an intimate relationship with the Lord. He knows the Lord for himself. He knows the worth and the value of prayer. A praying man has a hunger and thirst for God, His Word and the power of God. Praying men long to see God's glory as they do their work unto the Lord. Praying men energize and help other men. Praying men help to stir up REVIVAL! What a blessing it is to see a Praying Man. Praying men attack the gates of hell. Praying men are victorious through Christ. A praying man may fall but he knows how to seek the Lord to rise again.

Now when Daniel knew that the writing was signed, he went into his house; and his windows being open in his chamber toward Jerusalem, he kneeled upon his knees three times a day, and prayed, and gave thanks before his God, as he did aforetime.
Daniel 6:10

LIFE LESSONS

- A praying man covers and protects his family.
- A praying man is a blessing to the ministry.
- All men should pray and seek God daily.
- If you want to be successful then you should pray.
- Prayer is simply talking to God.

How Can You Be A Better Man?

1._____

2._____

3._____

4._____

Praying Parents

My husband tells everyone how he would see his mother pray. How she prayed for him day and night to turn his life over to the Lord. If she could see him now how proud she would be!

My mother would tell us how she would lay in the bed praying quietly waiting for her children to get in the house before curfew. If we were late my father would put the garbage can in front of the door and go to sleep.

They could hear us knock it over and know what time we came in. Mommy didn't sleep she prayed us in and sometimes moved the garbage can for us.

My father would always tell the story how our grandfather waited for the boys to get home. When my grandfather asked what time they got home my grandmother would say, "Early, they got home early." My father said it really meant early in the morning. Thank God for praying parents who intercede for their children.

As parents we have had many similar experiences. We prayed for our children day and night. We still pray for our children and our grandchildren. We pray for their salvation and for their mates. We pray that God will bless them and meet their needs. We pray for their relationship with God, for their protection, and we pray for the Lord to order their steps.

The best thing a parent can do is to pray. Prayer reaches our child when we can't for whatever reason.

There are many seasons and reasons that causes a parent to go into prayer mode. When you truly love your children and you love God you can't help but pray. Parents want God's best for their children. Sometimes a parent's heart aches for whatever their child is experiencing.

As Christian parents it is important that we teach and train our children how to pray and seek God for themselves. There will be many days when they will have to make their own choices and deal with difficult situations. They will need to know how to get a breakthrough from the Lord.

Right now our son is seven. He can be in the other room and hear you mention something. He will immediately come in the room and pray for you and with you and then walk out like nothing happened. He is just used to going into prayer mode. It is a part of who he is.

Recently our son had some issues in the school he was at. The decision was made to send him to another school. We prayed and we researched. We asked questions, we advocated and did all we could. It was a really tough time for us. God worked in the midst and gave us a peace in our spirit that we made the right choice.

LIFE LESSONS

- Lord, help us to make the right choices for our children.
- Help them to make the right choices for themselves.
- As our children grow and the circle of life continues help them to become praying parents.

How Can You Be Better?

1._____

2._____

3._____

4._____

Be Prayerful & Positive

We all have been through tough times in life. Some have had more hardships than others. No matter what you have gone through God wants us to become BETTER NOT BITTER.

God wants us to be Prayerful Positive People. It doesn't help any to go around blaming other people for our mistakes or to say what if? We can't live our lives based on WOULDA, COULDA, SHOULDA. It is what it is and we are where we are because of the choices we made in life.

God gets no glory when we are moody, cranky, selfish, bitter, angry, hard to get along with, mean, sarcastic, jealous and such; God gets no glory out of that. As Christians those things should not be a part of our character traits.

We should exhibit the Fruit of the Spirit **(Galatians 5:22-23).** God wants to use us for His glory. He wants His light to shine through us.

LIFE LESSONS

- When people meet us, talk to us, and spend time with us, they should come away feeling that they felt the love of Christ.
- Prayerful Positive People don't follow the crowd, they follow Jesus!

I Will Avoid Negativity

1._____

2._____

3._____

4._____

Pray First

And David inquired at the LORD, saying, Shall I pursue after this troop?
Shall I overtake them? And he answered him, Pursue: for thou shalt
surely overtake them, and without fail recover all.
I Samuel 30:8

I have learned the hard way just as many of us have that we need to pray
first before we make a decision. When someone presents you with a
question that requires an answer think it through, and pray about it first.
Look at both sides the pros and the cons if necessary. Don't rush, be
patient and wait for God to give you a peace in your spirit. When we rush
we can make the wrong choice.

I recently bought a new vehicle and the person told me that the first
vehicle I looked at was the only one in my budget. Even though it wasn't
what I really wanted I signed on the dotted line. I was on my way home
and realized I forget something. They told me to come back. I parked the
car and when I came back out the sun was on the other side. I looked and
looked again and saw a dent in the car. Long story short they took the car
back and I ended up getting the vehicle I really wanted in the beginning.

LIFE LESSONS

- God knows the hidden things that you don't know.
- Have to make a decision? Wondering what choice do you make? Seek
  God First?
- Ask God To Speak To Your Heart.
- Ask God to give you the wisdom and direction you need!
- Sometimes our spirit is saying, "No" but we are being pushed to say,
  "Yes". Don't do anything. Just wait until God says "Yes".

Plead the Blood of Jesus

Sometimes we deal with people and situations that get out of control. In one situation things became a little wild and crazy. I just started pleading "The Blood of Jesus." Don't you know all of a sudden it stopped, and things resolved.

When people come at you with craziness, you don't have to accept it. You have authority in Jesus name. You may not be in the place where you can pray and anoint with oil but you can surely pray in your heart and if need be break loose and plead the blood of Jesus.

When we plead the blood of Jesus it may be because of imminent or known danger. However the Holy Spirit can also lead us to pray and intercede. We pray the blood of Jesus for covering, protection, and direction. We trust God to intervene in whatever the situation is even though we don't know the details.

I remember hearing a story of a mother and father praying for their daughter who wasn't home yet. At the same time they were interceding, her car had broken down by the side of the road. The person helped her and her friend to get the car started and back on their way safely. **Read: Acts 12:1-19**

LIFE LESSONS

- It may seem old fashioned but, prayer still works.
- The blood of Jesus covers us all. Thank you Lord.

Listen to God's Warnings

Whenever I get behind the wheel to drive, I usually pray first or have someone in the car pray. The other day I was rushing. I had a lot on my mind. Just as I stopped at the gate for my house the Lord reminded me I didn't pray. I had stopped the car because of traffic anyway so I had my son (who was in the back) pray with me.

I checked the traffic it was clear. Then my son asked me a question. I turned quick to answer him and started to proceed. My mind said "STOP". I looked again and the side that was clear now had two trucks coming up. One after the other. There was no way I could get through. I needed to wait.

All I could think of was how glad I was that I listened to God's voice. Things can and did change in an instant. Always take time to listen to God's voice even if you don't know why. Always take time to look again.

Something similar recently happened to my husband. He was in the store and it came to him that he was going to lose his wallet in the store. As a result of hearing that in his spirit he adjusted his wallet when putting it away. He went on to his next errand. When he got to the cash register his wallet was missing. He immediately went back to the previous store. They insisted they did not find his wallet. Wondering what in the world was going on he went to get back in the car. When he opened the door he saw his wallet stuck between the seat and the belt.

He was happy he found it but wondered why it wasn't at the store. I couldn't explain it but all I could say is when God brought it to your attention you adjusted your wallet. Instead of losing it in the store it fell in the car.

LIFE LESSONS

- We may never know why things happen as they do but THANK GOD for him speaking to our spirit and giving us a warning.

Draw Closer

Lord, I thank you! Lord, I praise you! Lord, I give you all the glory and honor due unto your name. Lord, I worship you in the beauty of holiness.

Lord, help me to draw close to you today. I want to feel your presence. I long to please you and to worship you. You are my God. You are my Lord.

Thanking and praising you Lord for another day, thank you for touching hearts and minds and drawing us closer to you, thank you for opening doors that needed to be open and closing doors that needed to be closed. Draw nigh to God, and he will draw nigh to you.
James 4:8a.

LIFE LESSONS

- Thank you for teaching us, strengthening us and giving us hope and peace of mind.
- Thank you for souls saved and added to the church.
- Thank you. Lord, help me to live my life pleasing to you.

I Will Draw Closer

1._____

2._____

3._____

4._____

I Hear You Lord

God usually speaks to me when I am quiet. Quiet enough to listen. He may be speaking to me at other times too but when I am busy with other things his still quiet voice is crowded out.

Many times when everyone is asleep, or I am asleep God starts dealing with my spirit, showing me dreams, visions, showing me how to do a particular thing, bringing people to my mind to pray for, encouraging me to call and check on someone, giving me a word to share or bringing a scripture to mind to read.

Today I was home alone while my husband and son went shopping. I sat at my computer in the quiet house. I meditated on the goodness of the Lord. The words flowed and came to my mind. I typed them as the Lord gave it to me.

Thank You Holy Spirit. Thank You for speaking to my heart and to my mind. Thank You for anointing me today to write and to share.

LIFE LESSONS

* I know others will be blessed as they read this book because it is inspired by you.
* Thank You Lord!!! Thank You Jesus!!!

What is He Saying?

1._____

2._____

3._____

4._____

Setting the Atmosphere

Thank God for my honey. I'm in my office doing my morning devotion and he's in his office doing his. He's playing worship music. Lord, give us the mind and spirit to start the day in prayer, praise and thanksgiving.

When we start our day with Prayer, Praise and Worship, our day goes so much better. We love that song by Jonathan Nelson – 'Our Worship, Our Praise, is Shifting, Shifting the Atmosphere." It's true. If you want the atmosphere in your home to change start playing some anointed music.

My husband will also turn on the TV and walk out the room to do something else. At first I was wondering what's going on? You know we have to pay the electric bill! Then I realized what he was doing and one day he spoke with me and confirmed it. He was calling forth peace into our home through the Word of God. He was setting the atmosphere.

Joshua 1:8. This book of the law shall not depart out of your mouth; but you shall meditate therein day and night, that you may observe to do according to all that is written therein: for then you shall make your way prosperous, and then you shalt have good success.

LIFE LESSONS

- God knows the hidden things
- How do you start your day?
- What changes can you make to include some time with the Lord before you start your day?
- Lord, help me to meditate on your Word.
- Help me to find daily strength by searching the scriptures.

I Will Change the Atmosphere

1._____

2._____

Speak to Me, Flow thru Me

The Spirit of the Lord is upon me, because he hath anointed me to preach the gospel to the poor; he hath sent me to heal the brokenhearted, to preach deliverance to the captives, and recovering of sight to the blind, to set at liberty them that are bruised. **Luke 4:18.**

I always look for an opportunity to "Speak Life". The other day I was talking and I said something to my husband. He looked at me and said what are you talking about honey? I told him- "Oh sometimes I just speak into the atmosphere."

I believe in speaking those things that be not as though they were. I believe in exercising my faith daily. I believe in speaking life over myself, my family and any situation that tries to come against me. I speak life. I stand on God's promises and I pray God's Word.

LIFE LESSONS

- Speak life over whatever you are going through today.
- Holy Spirit speak to me, flow thru me.
- Give me the words to say.
- Use me for your glory in Jesus name. Amen.

Use Me Lord

1._____

2._____

3._____

4._____

Don't Walk Wounded

We can all probably imagine a time when we were hurt. Whether it was by a loved one, someone we loved, a friend or a "frenemy." We don't have to walk around nursing that hurt.

Today we are praying for those who feel wounded, hurt, cast down and have lost hope. Praying for those who need to overcome hurts.

Lord, help them to know that there is more to life. Help them to know that you have greater in store for them if they just reach out, ask you and trust you.

Encourage that person Lord, strengthen them in the name of Jesus. Help them to feel good about themselves and who you have made them to be. The blood of Jesus against any witch, warlock, demon or evil force that tries to come against us in Jesus name.

Praying Lord for those who are struggling in mind and in their spirit. Holy Spirit intervene in the situation. We bind all things unlike you Lord. We rebuke thoughts of depression, suicide, anxiety. The spirit of defeat and hopelessness are defeated. The devil is a liar. No weapon formed against us shall prosper.

No weapon that is formed against thee shall prosper; and every tongue that shall rise against thee in judgment thou shalt condemn.
This is the heritage of the servants of the LORD,
and their righteousness is of me, saith the LORD.
Isaiah 54:17

LIFE LESSONS

- Read your Bible daily.
- Replace those negative thoughts with God's Word.
- If you need to go and get counseling as well as prayer then do so.
- Lord, teach us how to love when we feel hurt.

Chapter 7

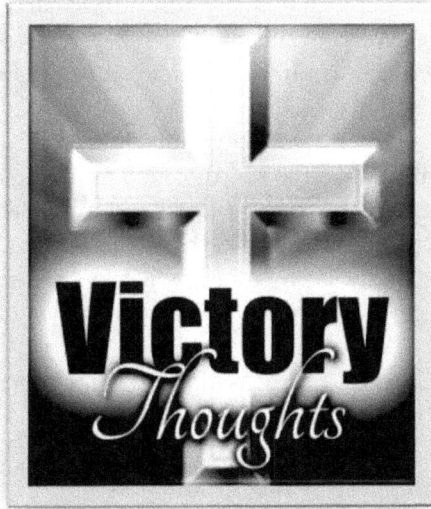

Spiritual Warfare

We must remind ourselves that we are not fighting flesh and blood.
We are fighting a spiritual battle.

The weapons of are warfare are not carnal but spiritual.

What Are You Thinking?

It's so easy to get distracted. Staying focused is of the utmost importance to get to the place God wants me to be. When things go wrong or we are anxious about something the enemy will attack our mind. Our mind is complex in nature. We can imagine whatever we want. Just as we can rehearse negative outcomes in our minds we can also rehearse positive outcomes.

It is important that we read the Word of God to help keep us on track. We must not allow certain thoughts to flood our mind. That is also why we should not only watch what we think but what we allow to enter through our eyes, and ears, and what we touch, where we allow our feet to take us and what we speak.

Lord, I need your help to stay focused. Lead me, guide me, direct me, and order my steps... In Jesus name.

Philippians 4:8
Finally, brethren, whatsoever things are true, whatsoever things are
honest, whatsoever things are just, whatsoever things are pure,
whatsoever things are lovely, whatsoever things are of good report;
if there be any virtue, and if there be any praise, think on these things.

LIFE LESSONS

- Lord, when I focus on your goodness, your mercy, and your grace, I can't go wrong.
- When I think of the goodness of Jesus and all he has done for me, my soul cries out "Hallelujah" I thank God for saving me.

Overcoming Depression

The enemy tries to keep us from being our best by speaking negative thoughts in our minds. Trying to weigh us down with worries, cares and drain us of our energy and vitality. There have been several times that I have battled the enemy in this area. For one year I took medication to keep me calm after experiencing a car accident, miscarriage and some other setbacks. Thank God He delivered me. I stayed in my room and wouldn't come out. God kept me and God brought me through it. My husband helped me tremendously. Every day I would do just one thing for myself. One thing that would bring me out of the dark hole that I slipped into. Yes, I was saved, sanctified and filled with the Holy Ghost. With my doctor's help, I weaned myself off the medication. My husband filled our home with the word daily. Morning, noon and night. The TV stayed on or the stereo played Gospel music. Slowly, I came back to myself. This time I was stronger. Now I can see when the enemy is trying to attack me and overwhelm me. It won't work. I know how to bounce back.

II Corinthians 10:4-5
For the weapons of our warfare are not carnal, but mighty through God to
the pulling down of strong holds; Casting down imaginations, and every
high thing that exalteth itself against the knowledge of God, and bringing
into captivity every thought to the obedience of Christ...

Isaiah 26:3
Thou wilt keep him in perfect peace,
whose mind is stayed on thee: because he trusteth in thee.

I Peter 5:7
Casting all your care upon him; for He careth for you.

LIFE LESSONS

- Make sure to get alone with God in prayer and praise.
- Cast your cares on the Lord daily.
- Do what you have to. Avoid burnout.
- Take a nap daily. Relax as needed.
- Do special things just for you.
- Use the tools you have to deal with life.

Making It through a Weak /Week Day

My father had a sermon that he would preach about "How to make it through a weak day. Not W-E-E-K but W-E-A-K." Looking back I can't even begin to imagine how many times God made a way for us as a family.

My dad went through a time when he was out of work. He went out and bought a fishing license then he bought each one of us a fishing pole. Many days we went to the beach and the park to catch our dinner as a family. Cleaning fish was not my favorite thing to do. Believe me.

During those days we ate lots of parsonage stew, spaghetti, government cheese and the government pork in a can. Leaders don't just arrive they go through a process of building and becoming. To be a leader you have to know "How to make it through a weak day." Whatever your weak day may be.

And he said unto me, My grace is sufficient for thee: for my strength is made perfect in weakness. Most gladly therefore will I rather glory in my infirmities, that the power of Christ may rest upon me.
II Corinthians 12:9

LIFE LESSONS

- How do you make it through a weak day?
- With Jesus I can make it.
- Thank you Lord I am victorious even on a weak day!
- Let the weak say "I am Strong".

Keeping It Together!

Did you look yourself in the eye today and tell yourself - "I'm going to make it!" There have been times when I felt weak and tired. Times when I felt like I just couldn't go on. Times when I needed to hear God's Word spoken to me to strengthen me and increase my faith. That's when I encourage and strengthen myself in the Lord. I tell myself "You are Victorious".

There are times when for whatever reason or circumstance you feel like you just can't take anymore. It's on days like those that we say a simple prayer- Thank You Lord for helping us to hold it all together... Thank You for Your strength!!! Thank
You for hope, peace and joy within.

Romans 10:17
So then faith cometh by hearing, and hearing by the word of God.

Isaiah 41:10
Fear thou not; for I [am] with thee: be not dismayed; for I [am] thy God:
I will strengthen thee; yea, I will help thee; yea,
I will uphold thee with the right hand of my righteousness.

1 Corinthians 10:13
There hath no temptation taken you but such as is common to man: but
God [is] faithful, who will not suffer you to be tempted above that ye are
able; but will with the temptation also make a way to escape, that ye may
be able to bear [it].

James 5:15
And the prayer of faith shall save the sick, and the Lord shall raise him
up; and if he have committed sins, they shall be forgiven him.

Romans 8:26
Likewise the Spirit also helpeth our infirmities: for we know not what we
should pray for as we ought: but the Spirit Himself maketh intercession
for us with groanings which cannot be uttered.

Stop & Take a Break

In times of conflict it's easy to respond with hate and anger but we must remember that change requires love, compassion and communication.

It's important to stop and take time to appreciate the little things in life. Decide to enjoy a day of beautiful sunshine, blue skies and warm weather.

Psalm 121:1-2
I will lift up mine eyes unto the hills, from whence cometh my help.
My help cometh from the LORD, who made heaven and earth.

Isaiah 40:31
But they that wait upon the LORD shall renew their strength; they shall mount up with wings as eagles; they shall run, and not be weary; and they shall walk, and not faint.

LIFE LESSONS

- Lift your arms skyward and drink in all the Vitamin D.

- Lord, help us to stop and take daily breaks.

- Help us not to get burdened down and overwhelmed by allowing ourselves to get stressed out.

- Thank You Lord for being the source of our strength.

How to Renew, Refresh, Restore

1._____

2._____

3._____

4._____

Menopause

Recently after surgery my body was forced into menopause. Here I was with a six year old (my miracle baby) and dealing with menopause. I was totally unprepared. I am a person who likes to ask questions and get answers. I asked my doctors for advice and the answer I received was to "Ask a friend. Everyone is different." Most of my knowledge came from searching the internet. I started having "Hot Flashes" and Insomnia. I sweated until my clothes were soaked.

It was not a pleasant experience. Not at all. I was gaining the weight back that I lost the previous year. I became cranky, irritable and moody to say the least. I'm still working on it. I'm better.

I know my triggers. One of the main keys is to take good care of myself. All those things I should have been doing all along. Eat right, exercise, get enough sleep...

I was standing on line at the store and the lady behind me was fanning and sweating like crazy. (The air condition was on and it was very cool). Her husband laughed and looked at the cashier and said – "She's having a Hot Flash." I looked at her and said – "It's ok! I have them too! We all laughed."

Galatians 5:22-23
But the fruit of the Spirit is love, joy, peace, longsuffering, kindness, goodness, faithfulness, gentleness, self-control.
gainst such there is no law.

LIFE LESSONS
- Lord, help me to exhibit the fruit of your spirit, especially when I am having a rough day.

"NO" and "Wait"

My son was hungry and wanted some cookies and milk. I was on my computer typing and wanted to finish my thought. He came and he stood by me and asked me to stop what I was doing and give him something to eat. I looked at him and said "Let me finish this and I will get it. I'll be right there!"

Now the cookies were in the pantry right across the hall and the milk in the fridge. He could reach the cookies but the last time he tried to pour the milk he spilt most of it so I understood why he was asking for help.

He began to have a tantrum which made what I needed to do prolonged. All I could think of is when God tells us, "No" and "We have to wait". How do we react? I eventually completed what I was doing and fixed his cookies and milk. I even added some grapes on his plate.

When we are waiting on the Lord our attitude makes a big difference. I have learned that it makes no sense to yell, jump, scream or have a fit.

Instead of pushing God away I seek ways to press in. I have found if I am busy helping someone else I have less time to think about being in a waiting pattern. If I am involved in encouraging and supporting others and doing the Lord's work I don't get caught up in feeling sorry for myself or anxious for an answer from the Lord.

Yes, sometimes God says "No" and sometimes God says "wait". He knows the reasons why. Things always turn out better when we make the choice to wait on God's timing.

LIFE LESSONS

- When God tells us "No" and "Wait" he tells us for a reason. Yes, He does know what is best for us.
- We may not think his reasons are good ones but he knows what needs to be completed before he can answer our request.
- Teach us Lord, how to act while we are waiting.

Chapter 8

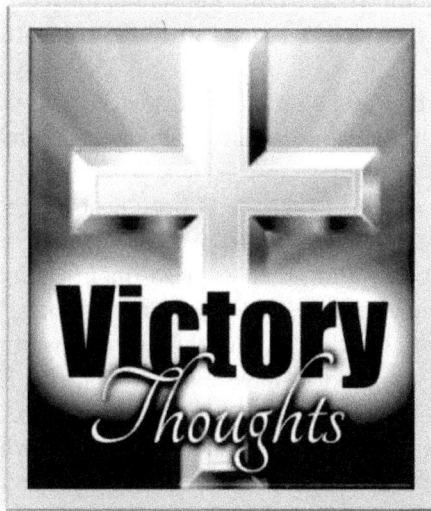

Walking & Waiting

Walking in faith means you not only know that God can,
but you know that He will. You wait in expectancy.
Knowing that God will move on your behalf.

Starting Where You Are

Today my thoughts went to my first car. It was a red hatchback that my dad bought for me for $500 from a mechanic. I loved the look of that car. Driving it on the other hand was a totally different matter.

The first inkling I had that something was wrong was when my car stalled in the rain in the drive through at McDonalds. I was embarrassed!

Someone helped me. They said the battery posts were loose. So I jiggled the posts and it started again. Later the driver door wouldn't open so I had to open the back, and reach over to open my front door. It didn't matter to me though because I was just happy to have my own car. I had spent so much time walking, taking the bus and waiting for someone to give me a ride. I was glad to have my own vehicle. Then there was the second car I owned that had a hole in the floor in front of the back seat and you could see straight through to the street when you drove. Of course I covered it over with a nice mat.

Then I had a beautiful car but the windows didn't roll down. One day as I was leaving work this car wouldn't go in reverse. I would have to put it in neutral, push the car back, jump in and drive. I got a good work out. It worked pretty well until the day it rolled in a ditch. Yes plenty of laughter remembering those days. In spite of all I went through I was thankful.

Do not despise these small beginnings, for the LORD rejoices to see the work begin, to see the plumb line in Zerubbabel's hand. **Zechariah 4:10.**

Thank God He blessed me with a good job and I bought a brand new car. It didn't have all the bells and whistles just the basics but it was brand new, it was mine and it was reliable. Since then God has blessed me with several new vehicles but I had to start somewhere.

LIFE LESSONS

- Don't despise the days of small beginnings.
- Lord you've brought me from a mighty long way!

God Still Opens Doors

Years ago I started working at a major newspaper company as a telephone operator. I wasn't making that much but it was enough. I really had a desire to go into journalism and figured it was a good starting point. In my spare time I started helping my father out doing bulletins, journals and typing for the church. I also did special projects for the clergy and ministers' wives and widows groups. As a result I created a pretty big portfolio.

One day while working I shared my dream of being a graphic designer with another telephone operator. She told me – Oh that's the so and so department. "You can't get in there even if someone dies. It's all old timers." I continued in that job for 2 years.

After 2 years I started praying seriously about where my life was headed and what was my purpose. A week later a posting went up for an Editorial Assistant in the newsroom.

I went on the interview and was told by someone that I wouldn't get the job it was already set aside for someone the interviews were just a formality. I went on the second interview anyway and I was able to speak directly to the Editorial department head who gave me advice. She looked at my portfolio and told me I needed more writing samples but it was a great Graphic Design Portfolio.

About 2 weeks later they posted a job for an Electronic Pre Press Operator (aka Graphic Designer). I put on my best suit and went for an interview with the director. He asked if he could hold my portfolio overnight. He returned my portfolio and asked me to call him back at the end of the week.

It was Friday and I couldn't wait to call. I was told he was in a meeting and would call me back. It was right before closing time I received a call. I was told that I was selected to be in the brand new department they were creating to change things over to computer graphics.

He proceeded to welcome me and told me I would start on Tuesday. I explained that my boss was on vacation and I needed to notify her. He said it's already taken care of I spoke with the director of the department and they have hired a temp to take your place. Wow!!! I was floored. I thank him and hung up. There was some crazy praise going on in my house that day!!!

Monday I went to work and notified my co-workers it was my last day. I was being promoted. Yes, God opened the door. My co-worker who said it would never happen just looked at me in awe while the others congratulated me. I worked on that job for 19 years. God used that job to bless me and then my family tremendously.

LIFE LESSONS
- What are you believing God to do in your life?
- Don't be discouraged! Don't give up!
- Be prepared and ready to walk thru the door God opens.
- People may tell you it can't be done that's ok.
- Believe what God has placed in your heart.

Doors the Lord Opened

1._____

2._____

3._____

4._____

Beyond What You See

Lord, lead me, guide me, direct me, order my steps, and show me the way! Speak to my heart. Have you ever had a time when you pay off one bill and another pops up? You take care of one thing and then another issue rises up trying to take hold of you?

It is in times like these that you have to continue to be faithful and consistent. Continue to believe God in the situation. No matter what you may see. I speak to myself and say "Thank You Lord my bills are paid. My needs are met. I am debt free."

Thank God for your new house even though the one you're living in now needs a lot of work. Thank and praise God for your new car even though you may be riding a bike, taking the bus, or begging a ride from a friend. Learn to pray and praise your way through.

I have a habit of making a list of my needs and desires. I bring them before the Lord in prayer. As the Lord provides I cross one thing off the list at a time. Sometimes more. Believe God first and watch God manifest it. Not only physical needs but spiritual as well.

LIFE LESSONS

- Write a faith list.
- Do you need a little more love, peace, joy???
- Start believing God for it to manifest in your life and in your home. On your job. In your spirit.

What Do You See?

1._____

2._____

God Will Make a Way

I can't even begin to convey how many times God has made a way for us out of no way. God has been good to us! We are truly blessed. Every 2 weeks I check my paycheck ahead of time to see what's going in my account so I can figure how much I have to work with.

Somehow I forgot to put in all my hours and my shift differential. Wow was I surprised when my pay check was little to nothing. The person who normally checks the timesheets was off and wasn't there to double check and make the necessary correction.

Thank God that we had a little elsewhere we could pull from to help take us through the next two weeks. I was upset with myself. I felt like it was my fault I missed it. I tried my best to stay focused and keep a good attitude. When the two weeks were over I received my back pay and also some additional sales pay. It was more than enough to do everything I needed to do. Thank You Jesus!!! I learned my lesson the hard way but God still worked it together for my good.

LIFE LESSONS

- How can you have a good attitude while waiting?
- What can you do to make sure you don't forget to do something important?
- God can give you more than enough!

How God Made A Way

1._____

2._____

3._____

4._____

Don't Doubt & Don't Give Up!!!

Don't believe the devil's lies. See yourself as God sees you. See yourself whole, healed, blessed, and working on a job you love, living in the house you desire, driving the car you need, married and happy with the family you desire.

I had just bought my home and I had not too long bought a new car. I used my refrigerator as my dream board. I cut a picture of a woman with her husband and family and placed it on the refrigerator door. I would update it with spiritual and motivational quotes. I would speak those things that be not as though they were. You may believe it but not yet see it. Keep praising and thanking God for the victory until it manifests.

One day we were having testimony service in church and I thanked God for my husband and family. It was a trip to see everyone's face as I spoke. My father (The Pastor) came up to me after the service and asked- "Do you have something to tell me?" I had no idea what he was talking about. He seemed serious and concerned. He said – "A husband and family?" I laughed. He was not amused. I said "Oh, I was just speaking in faith." "Oh, Ok" He said and walked away. It really was funny to me.

About year and a half later my husband and my oldest daughter came into my life. Don't doubt, don't give up. Wait on the Lord and watch HIM bring it to pass.

Psalm 27:14

Wait for the LORD; be strong and take heart and wait for the LORD. ...
Wait for the LORD; be strong, and let your heart take courage;
wait for the LORD!

I Won't Give Up!!!

1._____

2._____

Order My Steps Lord

When life seems like a maze know that if you seek God he will show you the way through. Then you will be amazed!!! Praise God!!! Thank You Lord for ordering our steps, leading us, guiding us and directing us in Jesus name.

I surrender all to you Lord. I submit to you Lord. Everything I am and everything I'm not. Use me for your glory, my strengths and my weaknesses as well. You are the Potter and I am the clay. Mold me, shape me, and make me. Only You Lord can change me into a new creation. Thank You Lord!

"O house of Israel, cannot I do with you as this potter?" saith the LORD.
"Behold, as the clay is in the potter's hand,
so are ye in mine hand, O house of Israel."
Jeremiah 18:6.

Trust in the LORD with all your heart and lean not on your own
understanding; in all your ways submit to him,
nd he will make your paths straight.
Proverbs 3:5-6.

God's Directions

1._____

2._____

3._____

4._____

Out of Your Box

You would be surprised at what you can accomplish. All you have to do is step out of your comfort zone and try. One day at a time one step at a time with Jesus I can make it. Yes, I can!!! Thank you Lord! Help me to be my own cheerleader. Help me to encourage myself in the Lord today!!!

When you take one step in obedience God will lead you step by step and bring you to a new place in Him.

That's what happened with this book. It started with one step of obedience. Just one step which led to another, and another and another.

When you step out in obedience God will propel you to the next level. He will supernaturally move you forward.

I can do all things through Christ who strengthens me.
Philippians 4:13

LIFE LESSONS

- Thank God for the people God placed in our lives.
- People who share their wisdom, knowledge and expertise.
- Learn to trust God one step at a time and step out of your comfort zone.

Thinking Out of the Box

1._____

2._____

3._____

4._____

Don't Get Bogged Down

God is blessing, moving and doing things in your life and ministry. You can see the next level approaching. All of a sudden out of the blue you start getting unwarranted attacks.

Make a decision not to get caught up in nonsense. Avoid gossip. If you have something to say make sure it's positive or say nothing at all.

Life Lessons

- Keep your eyes and your mind stayed on Jesus and what he has planted in your heart to do.
- Keep looking to Jesus the author and the finisher of your faith.

I Refuse to Get Bogged Down

1._____

2._____

3._____

4._____

Forgive, Heal, Move On

But I say unto you, Love your enemies, bless them that curse you, do good to them that hate you, and pray for them which despitefully use you, and persecute you... **Matthew 5:44**

When you have been hurt, rejected, abused, misused, embarrassed, or disrespected whatever it is, you need God to heal you from the inside out. Sometimes you just need to let it go and turn it over to Jesus. It sounds so easy and simple. Many people say forgiving is the easy part. Forgetting is another matter. Well you will have to learn to do both.

When you hold on to anger, bitterness, and resentment you become toxic. You poison your life and can't enjoy the blessings God has given you.

The best antidote for unforgiving and negative spirit is to exercise forgiveness. Forgive yourself and forgive others. Forgive, let God heal you and move on with your life. Stop wasting precious time.

No one likes being around someone who is miserable and self -absorbed anyway. Give yourself the gift of forgiveness. Open the prison door and set yourself free. In Jesus name.

LIFE LESSONS

- Lord, help us to forgive and then help us to forget.
- Help us to be better. Not bitter.
- Help us to forgive, heal and move on.

I Need You to Heal Me

1._____

2._____

I Got a Praise!!!

Have you ever start thanking God then it turned into praising God. The next thing you know you were lifting you're hands and worshipping the Lord. You opened your mouth and you start blessing the Lord, thanking Him continually lifting Him up and praising His name.

Thank you Lord for being my keeper, the lifter of my head, my friend... Thank you Lord!!! Lord, I praise You, I bless your name! Hallelujah! I thank You Jesus! Glory to your name!

I will bless the LORD at all times: his praise shall continually be in my mouth. **Psalm 34:1**
By him therefore let us offer the sacrifice of praise to God continually, that is, the fruit of our lips giving thanks to his name. **Hebrews 13:15**

LIFE LESSONS

- Lord, Thank You for healing, deliverance & making a way out of no way!!!

Thank You Lord!!!

1._____

2._____

3._____

4._____

I Am Free

God cares about what you are going through. Hear that? Feel that? Chains are being broken & people are being set free in Jesus name. Thank You Lord for bringing souls out from bondage, for setting people free from addictions, stress, worry, lack, hurt, dependency, fear, frustration... Yes, you are a delivering God.

I remember being in a situation which was causing me great stress. It was affecting me physically and emotionally. Finally, I made the difficult choice to move on. I had to be obedient and trust God for my future. It was a gigantic step of faith.

When I walked out the door for the last time I actually felt like a prisoned bird being set free. What a great feeling! Immediately I felt like a heavy burden had been lifted off of me. I had nothing but thoughts of hope, anticipation and expectation for my future.

Our soul is escaped as a bird out of the snare of the fowlers: the snare is broken, and we are escaped. **Psalm 124:7**

Come unto me, all ye that labor and are heavy laden, and I will give you rest. Take my yoke upon you, and learn of me; for I am meek and lowly in heart: and ye shall find rest unto your souls. **Matthew 11:28, 29**

And at midnight Paul and Silas prayed, and sang praises unto God: and the prisoners heard them. And suddenly there was a great earthquake, so that the foundations of the prison were shaken: and immediately all the doors were opened, and every one's bands were loosed. **Acts 16:25, 26.**

If the Son therefore shall make you free, ye shall be free indeed. **John 8:36**

LIFE LESSONS

- Thank You Lord for breaking our chains and setting us free!!! In Jesus name. Amen.
- Thank You Lord that I can turn to you.
- Thank you Lord I can find rest for my soul.

Sensitivity Training

There are many people who are seeking answers and looking for true authentic love. The Bible tells us to rejoice with those who rejoice and weep with those who weep. Take time to care about someone else.

When we are going through something we want everyone to be sympathetic. When someone else is going through we are quick to dismiss it. God wants us to be sensitive.

In ministry sometimes, we have to ask God to help us to not only hear what is being said but also what is not being said. This is an opportunity to share, to care, to be genuine and minister to the needs of others.

Sometimes people don't want anyone to help or they are not open to ministry. Just let them know we care, take time to pray, share a card, leave a message and move on. Once you have done what the Lord asked you to do, leave it there.

I Corinthians 3:6-9. I have planted, Apollos watered; but God gave the increase. So then neither is he that planteth anything, neither he that watereth; but God that giveth the increase. Now he that planteth and he that watereth are one: and every man shall receive his own reward according to his own labour. For we are laborers together with God: ye are God's husbandry, ye are God's building.

The fruit of the righteous is a tree of life; and he that winneth souls is wise. **Proverbs 11:30.**

LIFE LESSONS

- Lord, teach us how to pray and how to be sensitive to the needs of others so we may win them for you.

Who God Says I Am

For a long time I compared myself to others thinking I was less than because I wasn't exactly like someone else. That was until I realized God made me unique and an original is worth more than a copy.

You have to know who you are in Christ. You have to know your identity. There's no getting around it you have to immerse yourself in the Word of God and find out who you are and who you are meant to be.

If you don't know who and whose you are it will be easy for the gang to recruit you. If you don't know who you are it will be easy for the drug dealer to recruit you. If you don't know who you are it will be easy for any man or woman to speak into your ears and you believe what they say as they lead you down a deep dark path.

I Peter 2:9. But ye *are* a chosen generation, a royal priesthood, a holy nation, a peculiar people; that ye should shew forth the praises of him who hath called you out of darkness into his marvelous light...

I John 3:1-2. Behold what manner of love the Father has bestowed on us, that we should be called children of God! Therefore the world does not know us, because it did not know Him. Beloved, now we are children of God; and it has not yet been revealed what we shall be, but we know that when He is revealed, we shall be like Him, for we shall see Him as He is.

Read Deuteronomy 28:1-14

- I am blessed in the city
  and the field
- I am a winner
- I am more than a conqueror
- I am blessed
- I am healed
- I am delivered and I am set free.

LIFE LESSONS

- Know who you are in Christ.
- And all these blessings shall come on thee, and overtake thee, if thou shalt hearken unto the voice of the LORD.

Chapter 9

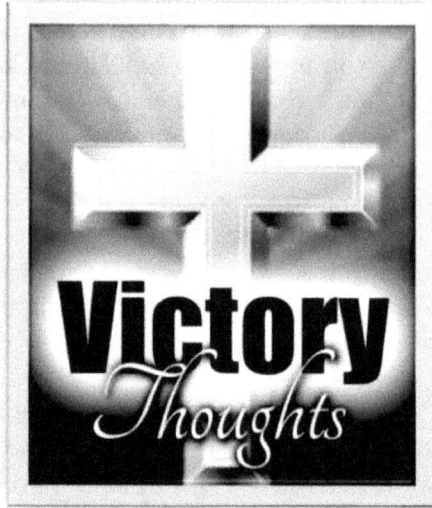

Walking in Victory

God wants us to walk in victory.
He wants us to be successful living our lives as Christians.

We want to take this time to speak into your life. Yes you reading this book! Whoever you are. It doesn't matter where you are. Near or far. Whether you are on your lunch break, in your car, getting ready for a meeting, taking care of the children.

No matter if you are sitting in a prison cell or whether you are in your own self-contained prison because of the choices you made. You may be in an abusive marriage, you may be in a bad relationship, and you may be in denial and trying to cope by hiding your pain with sex, drugs and/or alcohol. You may have uncontrollable anger which causes you to get into arguments with everyone no matter where you go. You may be feeling down because you are weighted down by bills and lack of finances. Whatever your situation is you first have to believe that you are going to come out of it.

Stop speaking and rehearsing that negative talk over your life. Read your Bible, listen to Christian television, find friends who are positive and Christ-like, and if necessary find a good Christian counselor to help you break the chains that are holding you back.

Jesus gave his life and shed his blood in order to win the victory for us. You don't have to walk around in life like a victim of your circumstances.

You may have been in the wrong place, at the wrong time, with the wrong people and doing the wrong thing but that doesn't define who you are. You may have made a mistake that tries to haunt you for the rest of your life. That is only if you allow it to. Your past is exactly that. Your past. Leave it behind you and don't look back.

Thank you for what you are doing in the life of our brothers and sisters. Thank you Lord for forgiving them, saving them, healing them and filling them with your Holy Spirit. Thank you for letting them know that they are not alone. Thank you for them seeing themselves as you see them. Thank you for ministering to their hearts and minds as they read your Word today Lord. Thank you for the positive, prayerful changes that you will make in their lives as they yield themselves to you. Thank you Lord that they will not hold back but they will give you every area of their lives. Thank you Lord for restoring those who have fallen. Thank you for giving them the strength to rise one more time. In Jesus name. Amen.

Victory Scriptures

In this chapter are some scriptures on personal victory that will help you as you grow stronger in the Lord. You can be the best person in the world. You can be nice to everyone but it's your relationship with Jesus that is going to make the difference in your life.

When I first accepted the Lord I would go to sleep with a notebook next to my bed. Every time the Lord brought something to mind I would write it down. You have to memorize and meditate on the scriptures so it will be in your spirit when you need it.

Psalm 119:11. Thy word have I hid in mine heart, that I might not sin against thee.

1 Corinthians 15:57 - But thanks be to God, which giveth us the victory through our Lord Jesus Christ.

Romans 8:37. Nay, in all these things we are more than conquerors through him that loved us.

2 Corinthians 2:14. Now thanks be unto God, which always causeth us to triumph in Christ, and maketh manifest the savour of his knowledge by us in every place.

Romans 10:38. Now the just shall live by faith: but if any man draw back, my soul shall have no pleasure in him.
Philippians 4:13. I can do all things through Christ which strengtheneth me.

Proverbs 15:22. "Without counsel purposes are disappointed: but in the multitude of counselors they are established."

Victory Statements

Sometimes we rehearse negative statements when we speak about ourselves. Try including some of these positive statements in your vocabulary daily. Let your words point you in the direction you want to go! Speak based on what God's word says about you and promised you.

I am blessed. I am healed. I am delivered. I am set free. I am a winner. I am an overcomer. I am more than a conqueror. I am growing. I am better, not bitter. I am stronger than I was yesterday. I am walking in faith. I am walking in victory. I will fulfill God's will and purpose for my life. I can and I will change. I refuse to give up. I won't give up. I won't turn back. I can do all things through Christ. I am the head and not the tail. I am above and not beneath. I am debt free. I am blessed to be a blessing. I may go through but I coming out. My life is getting better. I see myself as God sees me.

You get the idea! Read God's Word and Speak and expect VICTORY.

Life Lessons

- Let people know who you are IN CHRIST.
- When people try to label you and define you by your past let them know that you are a new creature IN CHRIST.
- Let them know God has changed my name.
- Don't call me by my street name.
- Don't call me according to who you think I am, call me by who God says I am.
- I am an overcomer. I am healed. I am victorious IN AND THROUGH CHRIST.
- If you need help put your pride aside and get the help you need.

What Changes Will You Make To Walk in Victory and Draw Closer to The Lord?

Chapter 10

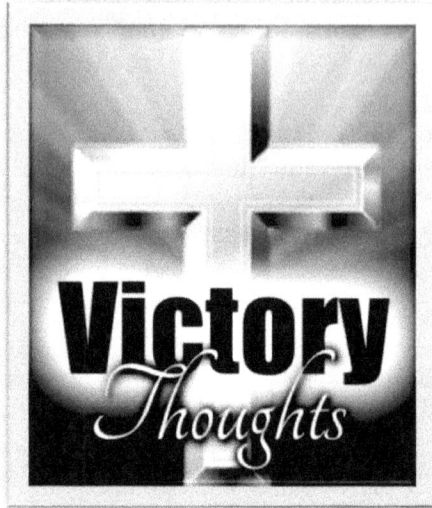

Victory Thoughts

Change your thinking and Change your life!

For as he thinketh in his heart, so is he...
Proverbs 23:7

Victory Thought #1
Thank you Lord for the blessing of family. Thank you for the people you put into our lives to love us, mold us, and shape us. Help us to realize and value the importance of family. Help us to live, learn and mature. Bind us together we pray thru good days and not so good days. In Jesus name. Amen.

Victory Thought #2
Lord, we thank you for the people you brought into our lives over the years. Thank you for the lessons you taught us thru example. Thank you for teaching us how to love and how to open our hearts and share with others. Thank you for instilling within us a desire to minister to others and spread your word in creative ways. Thank you Lord for touching the hearts, savings souls and using our family for your glory Lord. In Jesus name. Amen.

Victory Thought #3
Thank you Lord! Help us to realize that you can use ordinary things, ordinary people and ordinary situations for your glory! Help us to yield ourselves to you that we may open our eyes and see the opportunity for ministry all around us.

Victory Thought #4
Thank you Lord for the gift of encouragement. Thank you Lord for those people in our lives who freely share with us and look for ways to help us become better and stronger in you. Thank you Lord for those who plant seeds of kindness. Help us to be those who build and lift up others not those who seek to tear down and destroy others. Amen.

Victory Thought #5
Thank you Lord for friends. Thank you Lord for our neighbors and co-workers. Thank you for putting them in our path to share and be a blessing to them in some way.

Help us never to be ashamed to let our light shine and let others know that we love you and we are living our lives to please you. In Jesus name. Amen.

Victory Thought #6

Thank you Lord for those people in our lives who have the ability to see a need and help us. Thank you Lord for the people who do not look for acknowledgement. Those who want to serve and be a blessing. It may be a friend, a family member or a special person God has brought into your life for a time and a season. People who take the time to support others even in the smallest way are special and unique. If you have such a person(s) in your life take time to appreciate them. Many times if someone were to ask what we need we would say - "Nothing. I'm fine." God has placed people who can see beyond our walls and they don't have to ask they just meet the need as unto the Lord. Yes, Lord we thank you for such people. In Jesus name. Amen.

Victory Thought #7

Lord, we pray your blessings upon that person who is at a point in their life that they need to make a decision to move ahead. We thank you for speaking to their heart, leading them, guiding them and directing them. Order their steps. In Jesus name we pray. Amen.

Victory Thought #8

Thank you Lord for being our source. Thank you for being our provider. Thank you for being our way maker. Help us to know that all we have to do is ask you and trust you. You will provide for us. In Jesus name. Amen
.

Victory Thought #9

Thank you Lord for the 12 people who we will choose to encourage and pray for daily, weekly or monthly. We thank you for making the difference in their lives Lord. Whatever their need is Lord you know it. Be glorified in their lives Lord. In Jesus name. Amen.

Victory Thought #10

Thank you Lord for the lessons we have learned. We ask your blessings Lord upon that person who has gone through so much in life. Help them to be better and not bitter. Help them to look forward and move ahead. In Jesus name. Amen.

Victory Thought #11

Thank you Lord for helping us to learn from our children. Thank you Lord for teaching us to admit our mistakes and Thank you Lord for helping us to keep growing no matter what age we are. Amen.

Victory Thought #12

Thank you Lord for always making a way. Thank you Lord for teaching us how to handle our finances, how to stay in our budget, how to make good choices and how to be good stewards. Thank you Lord for helping us to teach our children how to do the same. In Jesus name. Amen.

Victory Thought #13

Thank you Lord that you have given us eyes to dream and see beyond what the physical eye can see. Thank you Lord for a heart that believes all things are possible with God. Thank you Lord for a desire to see more, do more, be more, and feel more. Thank you Lord for a heart that sees beauty where there once was sadness, for a heart that focuses on the positive and looks to the Lord for continued strength from day to day. Thank you Lord!

Victory Thought #14

Thank you that we can look beyond our losses. Lord, help us to realize that everything is not always going to go our way. Help us to change our focus. Help us to be teachers. Help us to be humble. Help us to celebrate ourselves but to celebrate others as well. Teach us how to work well with others Lord. In Jesus name. Amen.

Victory Thought #15

Thank you Lord that when we have to walk alone we will not fear. Thank you Lord for touching the heart and mind of that person who feels all alone. Thank you Lord for instilling within them the strength and courage to face another day. Thank you Lord for teaching them how to reach out to you in prayer. Thank you Lord for giving them a vision of a brighter and better days ahead. Amen.

Victory Thought #16

Thank you Lord for a spouse who loves me. Thank you Lord for our friendship. Thank you Lord for being with us through no matter the circumstance. Thru life, death, joy, laughter, tears, misunderstandings, sickness and so much more. Thank you Lord for a mate who loves you like I love you. Thank you for binding us together in love and in prayer only as you can Lord. In Jesus name. Amen.

Victory Thought #17

Lord, we thank you for dealing with our hearts to put you first in our lives. Help us Lord to always consult you first and foremost. Help us to never leave you out of our plans, decisions and choices. Lord, help us not to see you as an afterthought but an integral part of our life, relationship and ministry.

Victory Thought #18

Thank you Lord for the relationship with have with you and with each other. Thank you Lord that we can come together in prayer. Thank you Lord that you can unite our hearts and minds and bring us on one accord through prayer.

Victory Thought #19

Thank you Lord for a spouse who loves to worship you and give you the praise. Thank you Lord for my spouse who covers our family in prayer. Thank God for my husband who helps to set the atmosphere of worship in our home.

Victory Thought #20

Thank you Lord for bringing us through the times when we didn't see eye to eye. Thank you Lord for teaching us, training us, molding us and maturing us.

Thank you Lord teaching us how to love and respect one another. Thank you for showing us how to communicate with each other and listen to one another.

Thank you for teaching us when to speak and when to be quiet. Thank you Lord for teaching us the importance of forgiveness.

Thank you Lord for taking two strong people and blending us together.

Thank you that even when we disagree we know how to disagree without letting it escalate.

Thank you Lord for your Holy Spirit. Thank you Lord. Amen.

Victory Thought #21

Lord, we thank you and praise for love in its fullest. Help us Lord to show our love and passion for you as much as we long to please our mate. In Jesus name. Amen.

Victory Thought #22

Thank you Lord that we realize our limitations. Thank you Lord for teaching us to prioritize. Thank you for teaching us to use our skills. Thank you for teaching us time management and organization. Thank you for letting us know it all does not have to be done right now. Speak to my hearts Lord and let us know what is most important. Amen.

Victory Thought #23

Thank you Lord for the people who come into our lives as a result of ministry. Teach us how to share your love and give to others freely. Heal those who have been hurt and reluctant to reach out to others. Help our love to be honest, genuine and sincere. Give us wisdom and help us to walk in truth. In Jesus name. Amen.

Victory Thought #24

Thank You Lord! We know that you want the best for us and our family. Thank you for loving us and for teaching us how to love and appreciate one another.

Victory Thought #25

Thank you Lord for bringing us together and for keeping us together. Thank you Lord for making us whole. Physically, spiritually and emotionally in Jesus name. Amen.

Victory Thought #26

Thank you Lord that you can mend the broken pieces of our lives. Thank you Lord for fathers who truly love their children and do their best to take care for their children. Teach us as men to be responsible. Help us not to make excuses but to find ways to be there for our children. In Jesus name. Amen.

Victory Thought #27

Thank you Lord for our fathers. Biological fathers, step fathers, fathers in love, those who stepped in to mentor us and fill the necessary gaps. Thank you Lord for helping us to realize the importance and role of a father. Help us to heal broken relationships and move forward. In Jesus name. Amen.

Victory Thought #28

Thank you Lord for laughter in our home. Thank you Lord for the joy you give to us when we come together and just laugh. It costs nothing but it gives so much. Thank you Lord for the healing properties of laughter. Amen.

Victory Thought #29
Thank you Lord for excitement. Lord, help us to live our lives and share your word with passion and enthusiasm. Amen.

Victory Thought #30
Thank you Lord for letting us know who we are and where we come from. Thank you for giving us a sense of family. Thank you for giving us the mind to pass on traditions and information to our children.
It's wonderful to sit and look at pictures. Seeing the resemblance from several generations before. Telling stories. Laughing, crying and missing our loved ones.

Lord. Help us to teach our children about you and about the importance of family. Amen.

Victory Thought #31
Thank you Lord for Family Values. As old fashioned as it may seem to some help us to remember what is important in life. Help us to teach our children according to your word.

Victory Thought #32
Thank you Lord for those people you have brought into our lives as godly examples. Help us to keep our eyes open, to watch, to listen and to learn in Jesus name. Amen

Chapter 11

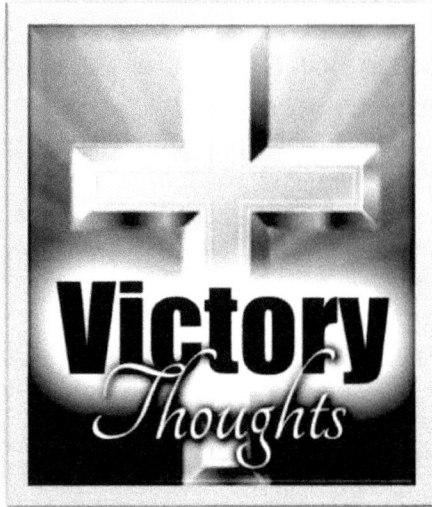

Have You Given Your Life to Jesus?

Jesus loves you so much that he gave his life for you!
Have you acknowledged that love?

Jesus loves you so much
He gave his life for you.

Oh, what a love.
True and everlasting love.

He never left you,
He is waiting for you
With open arms.

Won't you give Jesus
your heart today?

Don't wait!
Tomorrow may be too late!!!
The choice is yours!!!

Salvation

If you don't know the Lord as yet there's a simple way to get to know Him. Just by praying this prayer you will establish a relationship with Him. Father, I'm coming before you through Jesus Christ. I admit that I am a sinner. I am asking you to forgive me of my sins, cleanse me, and wash me. I believe that Jesus suffered, bled, died and rose again just for me. I believe Jesus showed His love for me to bring me back into a relationship with God the Father. I know that there is nothing I can do to earn your love. It is a free gift that God loved me so much that He gave His Son. Jesus loved me so much that He gave His life. I accept Jesus Christ as my personal Lord and Savior. I ask you to walk with me, lead me, guide me and order my steps. Now that you have prayed this prayer you are Born Again. You are a Christian and a child in the Family of God. We encourage you to read the Bible and pray to God every day and find a Bible believing, Bible teaching church to attend weekly. God Bless You!

Don't wait till tomorrow. Let Jesus in today!!!

John 3:16-17. For God so loved the world, that he gave his only begotten Son, that whosoever believeth in him should not perish, but have everlasting life. For God sent not his Son into the world to condemn the world; but that the world through him might be saved.

Romans 10:9-10. That if thou shalt confess with thy mouth the Lord Jesus, and shalt believe in thine heart that God hath raised him from the dead, thou shalt be saved. For with the heart man believeth unto righteousness; and with the mouth confession is made unto salvation.

Acts 4:12. Neither is there salvation in any other: for there is none other name under heaven given among men, whereby we must be saved.

John 5:24. Verily, verily, I say unto you, He that heareth my word, and believeth on him that sent me, hath everlasting life, and shall not come into condemnation; but is passed from death unto life.

Romans 1:16. For I am not ashamed of the gospel of Christ: for it is the power of God unto salvation to everyone that believeth; to the Jew first, and also to the Greek.

Chapter 12

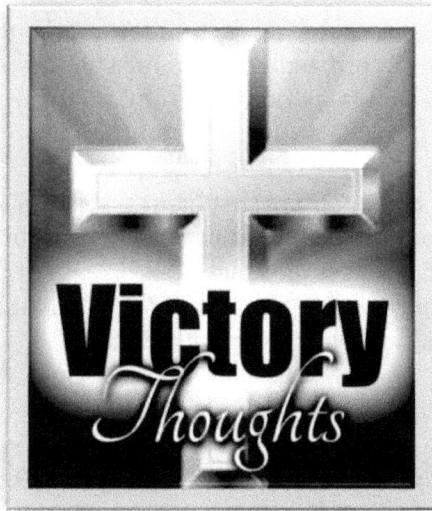

What Is Next?
Fight the Good Fight

God has a purpose and reason for each one of our lives. Something that he has assigned for us to do. Just us. The enemy's job is to try to stop us, block us, hinder us and deter us from doing God's will.

When we accept Jesus Christ as our personal Savior, the enemy is even more determined to discourage us, try to make us lose our testimony, try to get us to destroy ourselves through our actions and our thoughts.

In order to fight in the spirit we first must have the mind of Christ. We need to study God's Word and know God's Word for ourselves. We need to recognize when God is speaking to us and when the enemy is trying to deceive us.

This is a spiritual battle. Things first happen spiritually, in your mind, in your heart and then they manifest naturally. This works both for things that are good and not so good as well. We need to know spiritual principles and apply them to our lives. We can't do this unless we know God's Word and have a relationship with Him.

Many people think accepting Jesus Christ as your Savior is all there is to it. No, no, not so. You have to learn to fight in the spirit. To overcome temptation. To bind the hand of the enemy that seeks to kill you and destroy you. You have to know that Jesus came to give us life and life more abundantly.

Yes, you are a new creation in Christ but if you don't feed yourself the things of God you will die spiritually and end up in a backslidden state.

When you have accepted Jesus as your Lord and walk away to go back into a world of sin the enemy will try to pull the wool over your eyes. He will blind you into thinking that what you are doing is right. What a life! I have it all!

Meanwhile, it's more like a ferocious bull dog who has grabbed a hold of you and won't let you go until he destroys you.

The weapons of our warfare are not carnal but spiritual. We pray, we fast, we speak the word, we pray in the spirit.

Watch the news daily and you will see how the devil is ripping people's lives apart! Now you have to say to yourself what do I want for my life? Is

God pleased with my life, my ways, my actions, my thoughts? Is God getting any glory out of my life? How can I get closer to you Lord?

Living this Christian life is something you can't do alone. When someone is out in the streets and you hang with your crew or your people you become more and more like who you hang around.

When you are a Christian you want to be with people of like mind. You want to grow in Christ. You want to be around people who know Christ and want to be like him too.

Being involved in a local Church is important. Having a true Pastor to watch over your soul. Church School, Bible Study, Sunday and Weeknight services have proven to build me up in my faith. It's simple, you have to feed your spirit with spiritual food.

Fight the good fight of faith, lay hold on eternal life, whereunto thou art also called, and hast professed a good profession before many witnesses. **I Timothy 6:12.**

Ephesians 6:12. For we wrestle not against flesh and blood, but against principalities, against powers, against the rulers of the darkness of this world, against spiritual wickedness in high places.

Life Lessons

- Ask God to cleanse you, wash you, deliver you, heal you, and make you whole.
- Tell him Lord, I want to be real for you not tossed back and forth to and fro.
- Teach me how to walk in victory Lord.

A Final Word

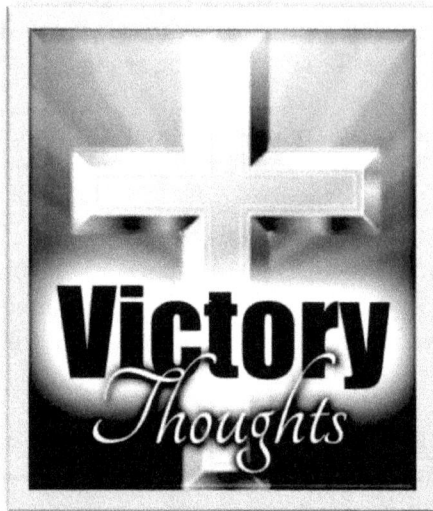

What is God Speaking to Your Heart?

This chapter includes space for you to write and share your thoughts. Make a note of what you want to remember. May God bless you and minister to your heart!

I must work the works of him that sent me, while it is day: the night cometh, when no man can work.
John 9:4

Sharing this body of work has made a difference in our lives. When you do what God has called you to do everyone will not comprehend it and that's alright! You still have to push and press forward in the name of the Lord! Some days you may feel all alone but know that God has spoken to you, that God has placed within you a vision for a time and a purpose. Know that the Holy Spirit is speaking to you and urging you to bring forth what the Lord placed within you before the Lord formed you.

170

It's like fire shut up in your bones. When you are obedient to the Lord and know that you are where He wants you to be and doing what He wants you to do the feeling is unexplainable.

The Lord brought us together as a husband and wife ministry team. He plants within us dreams and visions. He allows us to encourage and draw from each other. Proverbs 27:17 says - Iron sharpeneth iron; so a man sharpeneth the countenance of his friend. We bring out the best in each other and God uses that oneness for His glory! That how He works in our lives.

Now that you have read the book and taken a step further to write down what God is speaking to your heart. It is your time to go forth and complete the work the Lord has called you to do. What is your story? What is your testimony? What will be your legacy?

You may be young, middle aged or even a senior. You are never too young or too old to dream again. You are never too young or old to be obedient to the Lord and let Him use you for His glory!

Is your heart saying – "Yes Lord". "Show Me the Way Lord". "Lead Me, Guide Me, Order My Steps Lord".

Have you surrendered all to the Lord? All of your hopes, your dreams, your fears, and that thing which is holding you back?

Have you released your past, Have you trusted Him with your future? Have you given up your right to be angry? Have you released the bitterness and strife? Have you asked the Lord to cleanse you and wash you and set you free so He can increase and you can decrease?

Have you asked the Lord to take away the lying tongue, the evil look, the right to be right, and the need to make someone else suffer. Have you asked the Lord to open your heart and remove anything that you are holding onto that is unlike Him. It's as simple as saying – "Lord, change me". Giving our lives to the Lord is the first step. We then must move forward to walk and live in VICTORY!

What is God Speaking to Your Heart?

_____

_____

_____

_____

_____

_____

_____

_____

_____

_____

_____

_____

_____

_____

_____

_____

_____

_____

What is God Speaking to Your Heart?

But the path of the just *is* as the shining light, that shineth more and more unto the perfect day.
Proverbs 4:18

Share Some Love
House of Prayer Evangelistic Ministries Inc.

The Lord brought Elder Moses & Elder Vivian Johnson together giving them a heart for evangelism, missions and ministering to hurting people through the Word of God. We have a teaching, preaching and sharing ministry. We thank God for what He has done and look forward to what He will do in the future. Together they minister in Share Some Love House of Prayer Evangelistic Ministries which started as a home Bible Study in the year 2000 and was incorporated in June of 2013. The ministry has expanded to include the Website, Facebook Group and Facebook Daily Encouragement Page. They look forward to moving forward as the Lord opens doors and the ministry continues to grow. They have taught, preached and shared in many venues. One of the highlights of their ministry was serving as guest hosts of the New York TBN "Praise the Lord" Television show (Trinity Broadcasting Network). To God be the glory!!!

ELDER MOSES JOHNSON SR.

Elder Moses Johnson Sr. has been a Christian since October 17, 1979. He gave his life to the Lord during an open-air crusade in Kingston, Jamaica. He became a member of the Church of God of Prophecy at Maxfield Avenue, Kingston, Jamaica. After attending the University of the West Indies and University of Technology, both in St. Andrew, Jamaica, and Virginia Union University Theological Seminary satellite classes in New York State, Moses was ordained a minister in Mt. Sinai Baptist Church Cathedral. Elder Moses also taught remedial English and engineering science at Tivoli Garden High School in Kingston, Jamaica, and integrated science at Roosevelt Junior High School in Roosevelt, New York. Elder Moses Johnson Sr. resides with his wife, Elder Vivian, and youngest son Moses Jr. in Orlando, Florida.

ELDER VIVIAN MACKEY JOHNSON

Elder Vivian Mackey-Johnson is a PK (preacher's kid). Growing up as a pastor's child, she learned a lot about ministry. She gave her life to the Lord during a Youth for Christ Crusade at the age of sixteen years old on July 16, 1979. She is a preacher of the gospel. She has served in many leadership capacities in the church, such as missionary, teacher, praise and worship leader, choir director, church clerk, church trustee, and assistant superintendent of the church school. Elder Vivian worked as a graphic designer for nineteen years at a major newspaper. Today she is a licensed sales agent for health insurance and ministers to seniors. Elder Vivian is a loving wife, mother, and grandmother. She resides in Florida with her husband, Elder Moses Johnson Sr., and youngest son, Moses Johnson Jr.

Published by

Mackey Productions
"Catch the Vision of Victory & Never Give Up"

Moses Johnson Sr. & Vivian M. Johnson

Victory
Thoughts
Stories, Testimonies & Life Lessons

Also Available From Mackey Productions
RACE AGAIN
By Ronnie Weller

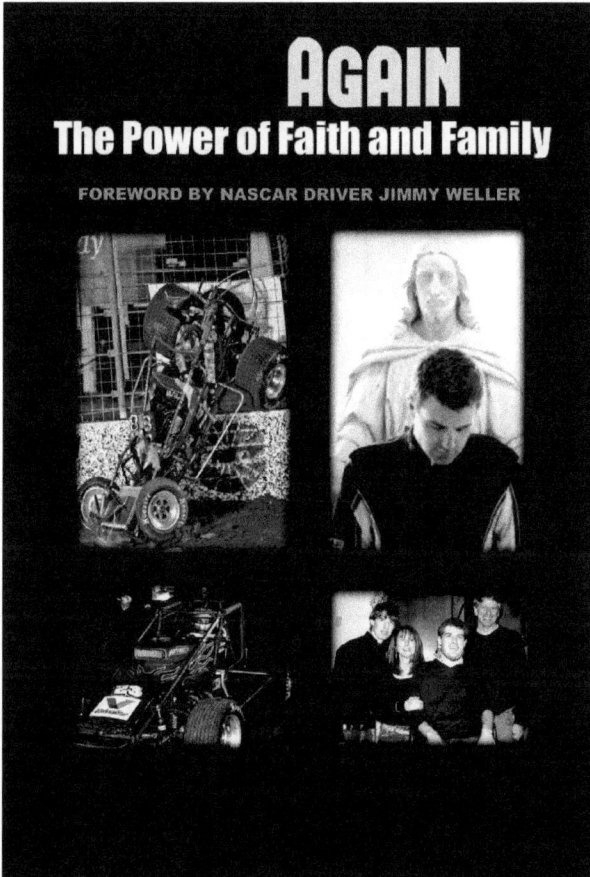

Also Available From Mackey Productions
A MINDSET FOR CHANGE
by Arthur Mackey

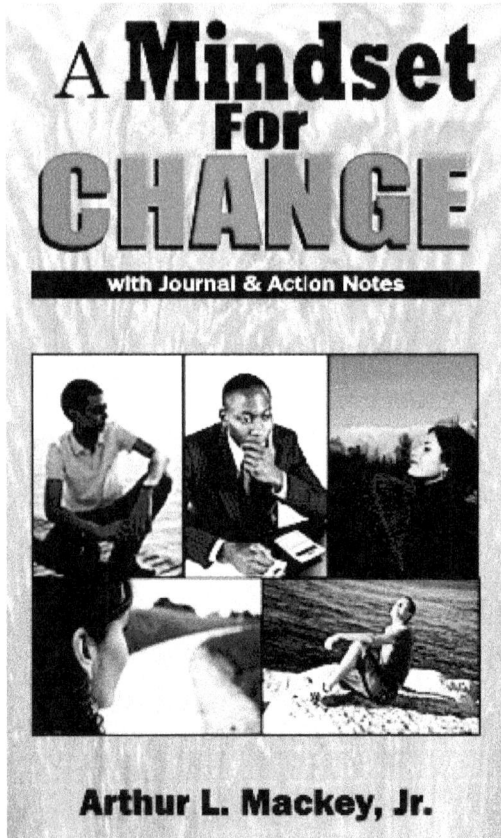

List Price: **$9.99**

ISBN-13: 978-1453615874
ISBN-10: 1453615873
BISAC: Body, Mind & Spirit / Inspiration & Personal Growth

Race Again by Ronnie Weller

Also Available From Mackey Productions
THE CALL TO COMMITMENT
by Arthur Mackey

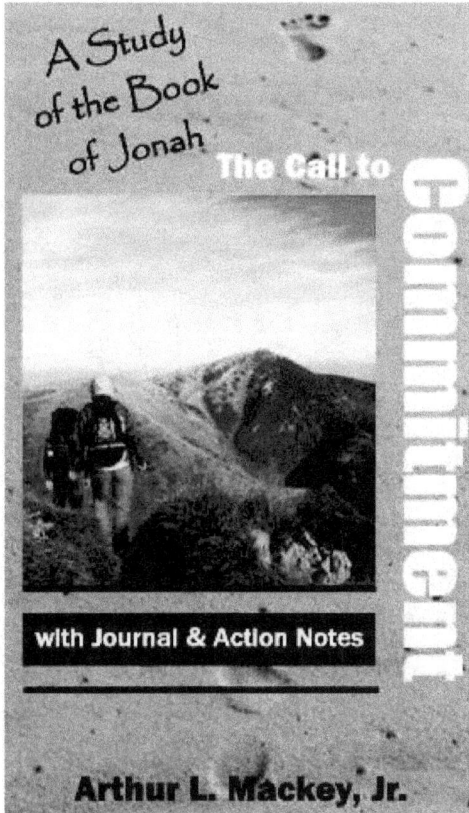

List Price: **$11.99**

ISBN-13: 978-1453686652
ISBN-10: 1453686657
BISAC: Religion / Christian Life / Spiritual Growth

Also Available From Mackey Productions
CHOSEN TO BE A SOLDIER
by Arthur Mackey

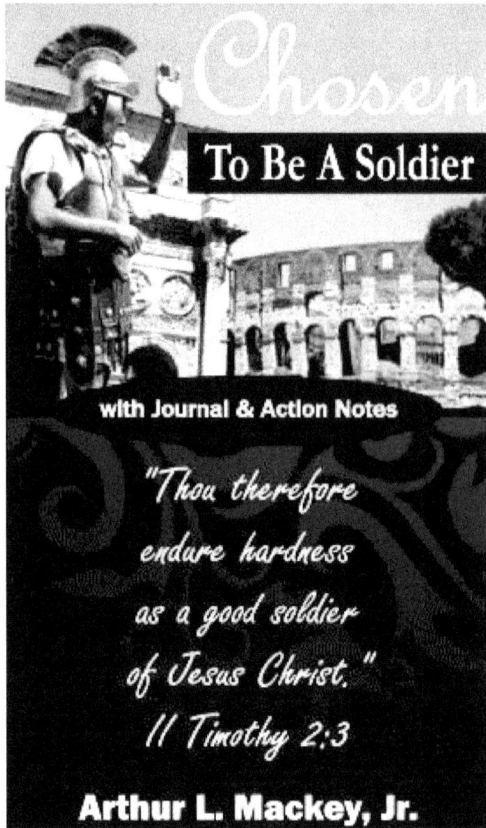

List Price: **$10.99**

www.ingramcontent.com/pod-product-compliance
Lightning Source LLC
LaVergne TN
LVHW051053080426
835508LV00019B/1850